JONAH:

The Anatomy of the Soul

by Stephen Goldberg, M.D.

MedMaster, Inc., Miami

ISBN # 0-940780-12-7

Made in the United States of America

Published by
MedMaster, Inc.
P.O. Box 640028
Miami, FL 33164

TO MY CHILDREN—
Shaani, Rivka, Marc, and Michael

CONTENTS

CONTENTS

PREFACE

I have written this book for several reasons:

A. As all people eventually die, they are faced with the question: Is death final or is there something, a mind, or "soul", that persists after the body decays? People often do not have religious beliefs to guide them on this question. Moreover, many cannot simply believe that reports of mystical "near-death" experiences in any way constitute evidence for life after death (such anecdotal reports may be exaggerated and simply reflect physiologic events in the body at times of great stress). One may also raise doubts over anecdotal reports of multiple lives and reincarnation. It would then appear that there is no answer to this issue. I believe there is another approach, as expressed in this book. It involves a closer examination of the nature and origin of consciousness.

B. Advances in computer artificial intelligence raise questions as to whether computers could exhibit conscious awareness. This book deals with this issue.

C. Physics, particularly the area called quantum mechanics, asks whether reality in our universe has something to do with the way we observe events, whether we are conscious of them. An understanding of consciousness will help in exploring these ideas.

D. There are times in one's life when one struggles with questions of whether there is purpose in the universe, whether the course of the universe is determined or whether there is a capacity of people and God, if there is one, to change things through human free will and higher level intervention. The question of free will is very much intertwined with the nature of consciousness.

E. This book is for my children, so that they may know the thoughts of their father, when he was not collecting baseball cards, or playing video games or ping pong with them.

Rather than using pedantic and difficult language in discussing complex issues, I have presented this discussion in a story form, using Jonah in the Whale as a parable. The reasons for selecting Jonah should become clearer as the book progresses.

Specific questions discussed in this book are:

1. What is consciousness?

2. How does consciousness arise? What is the relationship between consciousness and the brain?

3. Does consciousness persist after death?

4. Can a computer be conscious?

5. What is the relationship between consciousness and information; between consciousness and quantum phenomena; between consciousness and time and space?

6. Could creation occur from zero?

7. Does free will exist?

8. What is meant by "God", in a scientific sense?

9. If there is a God, can God influence the world?

10. What is the endpoint of evolution?

11. If God exists, why does God allow evil to exist?

I thank Stefano DiMauro, Ron Fisher, Phyllis Goldenberg, Jeff Hirsch, B. D. Josephson, and Jeff Klein for a number of critically helpful discussions.

Stephen Goldberg

INTRODUCTION:

The Definition of Consciousness in This Book.

The literature uses the word "consciousness" in different ways. It is important to specify at the outset the specific usage of the word in this book. BY "CONSCIOUSNESS" I REFER SIMPLY TO "RED", THE "SMELL OF COFFEE", THE "FEEL OF A PINPRICK", THE "TOUCH OF A FEATHER", THE "SOUND OF A TRUMPET", THE "TASTE OF HONEY", THE "FEELINGS OF LOVE, HATE, FEAR, ANXIETY, CALM, ETC." I refer in all these cases to the actual *feeling* that an individual has rather than to any neuronal or other processing that may accompany it. If one were to examine the brain closely while someone contemplated the smell of coffee, the examiner would not find coffee. The examiner might find particular neural circuits that fire in particular spatiotemporal patterns at the time the person contemplates "coffee", and the examiner might even find, after injury of these circuits, that the individual no longer reports the smell of coffee. There is some kind of correlation between the circuitry and the experience of the smell of coffee. It is the actual feeling, or experience, of the smell of coffee, as opposed to the circuitry involved that I refer to as "consciousness" of coffee.

I will use the term "consciousness" as synonymous with the word "awareness." By "consciousness" I do *not* mean "awareness of awareness." "Awareness of awareness" refers to a person's being aware of the fact that he is aware (conscious). Yesterday, for instance, I saw the color red, but I never once stopped yesterday to say to myself "Say, I not only see that color red, but I'm aware that I am aware of this color." I was con-

1

scious (aware) of red yesterday, even though I never was aware that I was aware. It is the simple sense of the meaning of "consciousness"—just plain "awareness"— that I will use.

The term "consciousness" should be distinguished from certain uses of the term "mind." "Mind" sometimes is used to portray relatively complex intellectual functioning, whereas "consciousness" may be relatively simple (e.g., consciousness of a pinprick). Moreover, in another usage of the term "mind," namely the "subconscious mind" (similarly, a "subconscious thought") one can conceive a mind (or thought) that lacks consciousness. If at times in this book I do use the term "mind" (or "thought"), it will be used synonymously, unless otherwise indicated, with "consciousness" and "awareness."

The term "consciousness" should be distinguished from the term "life." Organisms that exhibit organization, respiration, irritability, movement, growth, reproduction, and adaptation are said to have "life." There is nothing intrinsic to "life" that presupposes the existence of consciousness. Conceivably, a vegetable may be alive but not be conscious of anything. The question of whether a computer may be "alive" is a lot different from the question of whether a computer can be "conscious." This book discusses the issue of whether a computer can be conscious. The term "consciousness" is related to the term "soul," although "soul" commonly refers to the sum context of an individual's conscious and unconscious mind, and more, often carrying other spiritual connotations, including the presumption of its persistence after death.

PART I.
Consciousness

CHAPTER 1.

THE STORM.

The roll and roar, the rhythm of the waves echoed something from the far, far past, something powerful yet soothing, something cyclic, something secret.

The year was 1992. It was a beautiful sunny day, and Jonah lay on the sand. He reflected on his future. What should he do with his life? He had an inner calling to accomplish something useful for CIVILIZATION. He would spread peace and love, and make everyone happy. Perhaps, as each cell in the human body had its function, he also had an important function in the great body of the universe. Alternatively, perhaps he lived in a meaningless universe in which one's actions were predetermined or otherwise unimportant. What could he do anyway within the narrow range of his abilities? He was a molecule within a sandgrain on a vast beach. He could not make waves. These thoughts only depressed Jonah, and he dismissed them. And Jonah slept.

In his dream, Jonah was a passenger on a ship. He was saddened because he felt he was not fulfilling a mission in life, and was even unsure as to what his mission, if any, was. A great storm then arose, placing the ship in great danger. This storm was most peculiar. It appeared to affect only Jonah's ship and not other ships in the vicinity. Sensing the aberrant nature of the storm, the crew asked among themselves whether it was a natural phenomenon or had some supernatural origin. Sudden storms at sea were not uncommon. It was possible that a storm's center could have a narrow focus and involve only their ship.

But the unlikelihood of this explanation became increasingly apparent, as they tried to steer their ship from the vicinity but still found that the storm followed their ship and left the other ships alone. Weathermen on the ship determined that the general wind speeds and shifts of the storm appeared natural enough. The storm could be attributed to natural factors that coincidentally focused the storm on their own ship. There were no natural variables that they could see that would otherwise be responsible for the events. It could have been coincidence. But, the longer the situation persisted the more the crew became uneasy with this explanation. It was the predictability of the storm's movements that began to suggest some other factor than coincidence as the cause of the situation. The ship was the same one they had been accustomed to sailing for many years. It carried no unusual cargo that might attract or affect the course of a storm.

As the storm worsened, the crew members grew more fearful. They guessed that someone on the ship may have been responsible for the storm. They drew straws with the vague hope that this might clarify who the culprit was. Jonah drew the short straw. A single trial, though, did not convince the crew of anything. *Someone* had to pick the short straw. Even if there were billions of crew members, someone had to pick the short straw, and when that person did, it would not be an unexpected sort of result. Why should they assume that Jonah had anything to do with the storm? However, they drew straws again and again, each time with the same result. The more trials that ended with Jonah, the more the crew suspected, although they couldn't be sure, that something more than ordinary coincidence was at play. Something appeared to be influencing the results.

The storm yet worsened and the crew had to make some decision, and fast. Should they get rid of Jonah? He had appeared sullen and strangely silent ever since the voyage began. Maybe he knew something of these events. They questioned Jonah.

Was there something he had done that may have caused these troubles? Jonah told them that he had been feeling depressed and perhaps a bit guilty about not finding and carrying out his calling in life. This further alarmed the crew.

The greater the *unexpectedness* of an event (the storm following the ship; multiple trials of straw selection, always ending with the same person), and the greater the *meaningfulness* of the event (in this case the idea that Jonah may have done something wrong) the more the crew was inclined to look for a supernatural cause, rather than random forces. They linked Jonah to the storm. But how? All these events did not in themselves imply that Jonah caused the storm.

There was something ominous about Jonah, but they were still reluctant on these observations alone to throw him overboard. As a test they placed Jonah partway into the water, and the storm lessened. They withdrew him and the storm strengthened. With that, the crew was now on the verge of thoroughly dispensing of Jonah. Jonah was responsible for the storm. But still there was some last-moment reluctance, for they were about to embark on an act of murder. They did feel they had sufficient evidence to form a hypothesis that Jonah's presence or absence on the ship was correlated with the severity of the storm. They reviewed these considerations, before making a final decision. One crew member remarked that this may be a deterministic universe, in which all events, including all the events they had witnessed, were determined at the moment the universe originated. How could they then blame Jonah? Whatever so-called "evil" acts he may previously have engaged in were beyond his control.

Counter to this argument, however, was the reply that if this were a deterministic universe, the crew's actions were also predetermined, and the crew could not be held responsible for its own actions. So why not throw him overboard?

But what if this were a nondeterministic, universe, in which there were free will?

But, if so, was Jonah's behavior sufficiently bad to warrant the crew's killing him?

They did not know, but concluded that unless they removed Jonah from the ship, they would all die, and it was better to have him alone die than for everyone to die. And with that thought, they threw him overboard. They did not wish to take chances.

CHAPTER 2.

THE WHALE SWALLOWS JONAH.

What Distinguishes Reality, Dreams, and "Existence After Death"?

As Jonah dropped into the churning sea, he instinctively panicked. His entire life flashed before him. As he sank, his struggling limbs began to slow. Both he and the water became calmer. A weightless, tranquil sensation overcame him. He felt at one with the universe as he was swept along a long tunnel toward what appeared to be a distant and pleasant, peaceful, bright light.

Then, a sudden snatching motion engulfed him. Jonah was in the bowels of a huge whale. Jonah tried to orient himself while shaking off his dizziness. It was not just an ordinary whale, but a transparent whale within which he could move about freely, shrinking or enlarging himself, and searching as he wished.

Jonah assessed his situation. Was this real? Was this a dream? Was he dead? How could this bizarre situation be real? But then again, it *felt* real. He had always distinguished his dream world from the real world by the fact that he always seemed to wake up from the dream world in his bed in the real world. The real world also seemed so much more continuous, and "real." But would he wake up now? How long would this world have to persist before he could know whether this were real or if he were dreaming — or dead?

Jonah had no idea as to what happened after one's death. Like most people, he had never thought much about it. This experience was, at the very least, a near-death experience. He had heard that other people who had had near-death experiences reported similar experiences such as peace and floating and a tunnel that flowed toward a distant peaceful bright light. It was certainly nice to know that just short of death their experiences were pleasant, but what evidence was there that such experiences in any way reflected events that occurred *beyond* death?

Just because a person's heart stopped, or respirations stopped did not mean death of the brain or the person. That was a primitive concept, a throwback to the times when one assessed death by the best means available — evaluation of heartbeat and respirations. That is, in the past, people whose heartbeat or respirations stopped were noted, after a suitable period of waiting, not to come back to life, and it was supposed that loss of these functions was synonymous with death. People who have had terrible scares have been known to have similar "near-death" experiences, short of actually dying. The soldier who has suddenly lost a limb on the battlefield, and experiences "battle shock" may have an experience of tranquillity and lack of pain. Perhaps the pleasantness of near-death experiences does not reflect an afterlife but simply is an adaptive physiologic mechanism of the body that enables it to cope with great stress, as in the condition on the battlefield. Jonah was a skeptic, a depressed skeptic. While not challenging the existence of near-death experiences, i.e., the knowledge that near death there may be a very pleasant experience, he wondered whether certain aspects of such anectdotal reports were exaggerated to give people the idea that the experiences reflected life after death. People want to believe in an afterlife and may give unwarranted interpretations to the significance of the near-death experience. Jonah did not know whether he was in the real world, whether he was dreaming, or whether he was dead, but his suspicion that he was not dreaming became greater as he continued to note that he was not waking up and his adventure was proceeding in a rather real-appearing and continuous fashion.

The thought of this being the real world was unsettling, for if this were real, he was in imminent danger of dying. He asked himself, more seriously than ever before, whether death was final or whether something lay beyond. Was there "life after death"? Being neither inclined to accept answers on the basis of faith, nor inclined to have anything but a skeptical interpretation of near-death reports, Jonah got nowhere with his reasoning. The question was unanswerable — seemingly.

The stress of these events and thoughts exhausted him. And Jonah slept.

CHAPTER 3.

JONAH DREAMS OF TWO PLANETS.

Which Is More Desirable: "Life-After-Death" or "Consciousness-After-Death"?

Jonah dreamed of two planets that had two different courses of evolution. On one planet, life derived from simple molecules. Chance combinations of molecules formed new molecules, some of which were unstable and disappeared. Other molecular combinations were more stable, and, in particular, one of these molecular combinations had the ability to reproduce itself, thus allowing not only its persistence but its duplication and wide distribution. Chance variations of this molecule also had the same reproductive qualities.

More complex combinations of molecules developed into molecular conglomerates with such life functions as organization, respiration, irritability, movement, growth, reproduction, and adaptation. Some of these molecular conglomerates had only one or a few of these qualities. Some had all of them. Some conglomerates became cells. Cells combined to become organisms, with the eventual appearance of an advanced human-like organism. At the end of evolution on this planet, there was a continuous spectrum of life ranging from the molecular all the way through man with all permutations of life qualities that one could imagine, from simple to complex.

The residents of this planet did not have a word for "life." The word had no meaning, for there was nothing that absolutely separated "living" from "non-living." Everything was a continuum from molecules to man. If someone were to call one end of the range "alive" and the other "dead," where would the transition lie?

The second planet was Earth. Evolution proceeded in a similar way except that at the end, there was a huge gap between the molecular and the human. In fact, things in the world seemed to be grouped very close either to one end or the other of the spectrum. Sensing these two groups, people invented the term "Life" to distinguish the more advanced end from the molecular end. Some people even thought that there was a mysterious, supernatural difference between objects in one group as compared to the other. In time, though, more and more things were discovered, like viruses, that had characteristics in between the two groups. Were they alive or dead? It became a semantic issue. There really was no absolute meaning in calling something alive or dead. In reality, if one wished to use the term "life," everything had life but it was only a matter of degree. Otherwise, where would one draw the line between life and death?

Jonah thought about this and decided that he would have to redefine what he really wanted to ideally experience after he died. Did he wish "life after death"? If "life" were just a semantic term, and everything from the molecule through the human were alive, albeit to different degrees of complexity, then he would not be satisfied with just "life after death." The level of *complexity* of life would have to be high enough so that he would still resemble Jonah. Jonah, though, had another, more significant problem with desiring "life after death." He imagined himself fully alive but not conscious of anything, like a robot that performed the same complex mental and physical gymnastics as he but was not conscious of anything. This prospect greatly displeased him. Consciousness was all-critical to him. Even if his body were to disappear, he would like to have his consciousness persist. He did not want to be an intelligent, but unconscious robot. A persisting consciousness was more important to Jonah than persistence of the semantic entity called "life." He couldn't take "life" with him anyway, if "life" implied the physical functioning of his body, which was sure to decay. If Jonah had one thing that he wanted to take with him while his body decayed, it was his conscious mind.

But does not consciousness also disappear with death?

CHAPTER 4.

JONAH CONVERSES WITH THE WHALE'S BRAIN.

What is Necessary for Consciousness to Exist? Does Consciousness Persist After Death?

What Jonah really wanted after death was persistence of his conscious mind. But this appeared to be impossible. After all, wasn't consciousness contingent on the presence and functioning of the brain? Brain destruction means unconsciousness, coma. Surely his brain would decay with his death and that would mean the end of him and any prospect of consciousness.

But Jonah thought further. What was consciousness anyway? Did brain functioning somehow *produce* consciousness? If the brain did produce consciousness, how did consciousness get back to the brain to let it know about it, to tell other people about its consciousness? And what was so special about the brain that made it so uniquely associated with consciousness? Yes, what was so unique about certain brain areas, like the *cerebrum*, that we call "conscious", as opposed to other areas, such as the *cerebellum*, which when stimulated do not give rise to conscious experiences, and which are commonly called "unconscious"?

At that moment, a voice arose within the whale's brain. It was the whale's cerebellum, and it began to speak to Jonah. "Jonah," said the whale's cerebellum, "I believe you are under a misconception about what consciousness is and the conditions that are necessary for the existence of consciousness. I am conscious."

Jonah was taken by surprise. It was not a talking cerebellum that surprised him so much (for after all, such things can happen in a dream world), but it was the content of the statement. How could a cerebellum be conscious? Jonah, who had a cerebellum of his own, never recalled being conscious of its functioning. Brain scientists believe that the cerebellum acts in an "unconscious" way because it continually regulates numerous finely detailed actions of the hundreds of muscle groups in the body without the person ever becoming aware of this multitude of complex functions. Jonah was not only unaware of these cerebellar functions but was *glad* he wasn't. If he were conscious of all his cerebellar activity that was involved in the movement of a finger, he wouldn't have time to think about anything else. He constantly would be in a frenzy, trying to juggle the innumerable neurophysiologic events that are involved with every slight action.

The whale's cerebellum continued, though. "It is not only I that am conscious, but all other areas of the body, even your liver, are conscious also."

Jonah protested. He pointed out that he was not conscious of any functioning of these organs in his own body. If one were to remove his liver or kidneys, he would still be just as conscious. These organs were unconscious!

The cerebellum then proceeded to raise certain points that began to change Jonah's perspective.

First, the cerebellum pointed out, if it were true that the cerebellum is not conscious and the cerebrum ("the seat of consciousness") is, what is it that distinguishes them physically? They both consist of nerve cells and nerve connections. What real difference exists that would account for such a radical difference in being "conscious" versus "not conscious"? (fig. 1)

Jonah had difficulty with this question, but it was not enough to change his objection. Jonah first supposed that the cerebrum might be more complex in some way than the cerebellum or liver and that, somehow, complexity had to do with the issue. This argument was challenged by the cerebellum, which pointed out that both the cerebellum and liver perform quite complex functions. The "subconscious mind" can also perform quite complex functions. Moreover, relatively simple sensations,

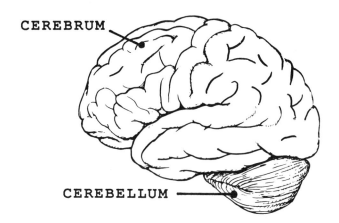

CEREBRUM

CEREBELLUM

Fig. 1

like a pinprick, can achieve conscious proportions. Jonah countered, however, by considering that a "simple" pinprick may in fact contain more elements of complexity than might at first be apparent.

The cerebellum then pointed to another, perhaps more noteworthy, difficulty in attributing consciousness to the degree of "complexity" of function: If one had to reach a certain level of complexity to achieve consciousness, what would be the cut-off point in complexity between conscious and non-conscious? Would there be some mystical critical level of complexity at which consciousness suddenly arose? Does it not make more sense to think of consciousness as a continuum from simple to more complex than to think of it as an all-or-none phenomenon?

The cerebellum then delivered its final and critical argument: "Jonah," said the whale's cerebellum, "*You are a highly complex conscious individual. You are inside this whale. If complexity is the issue, why is the whale not conscious of your thoughts? You and I have the same difficulty in communicating with the whale. The whale is full of conscious Jonahs, and these include you and me. You are also full of conscious Jonahs.* We are so arrogant as to think that we have but one mind. Actually, what we have been used to thinking about

19

as subconscious, or unconscious functions are actually conscious functions of separate Jonahs in our bodies."

This thought staggered Jonah. He pictured himself sutured to the whale's brain, with the whale still unaware of his thoughts. It did, after all, make more sense to think of all areas of the brain as being conscious, but to different degrees, than to think of certain areas as being unconscious. If one thought that only certain areas were conscious, one would be faced with the difficulties of explaining what physical qualities distinguished the unconscious areas from the conscious ones. It made more sense to think of consciousness as a continuum from simple to complex than as an all-or-none phenomenon. But if consciousness is a continuum, then why should a person be so *totally* unaware of his cerebellar functioning? Should he not at least be *partially* aware of it, as well as aware of the functioning of many other areas of the body that are classically considered unconscious? The fact that a person is so *totally* unaware of cerebellar and other complex functioning suggests that the situation of the cerebellum and other "unconscious" organs is more like Jonah-in-the-whale. There is consciousness associated with the cerebellum but the person is unaware of it just as the whale is totally unaware of Jonah's thoughts.

This still left Jonah with an unsettling question: If his cerebellum and other brain areas were all conscious, why is it that *he* didn't know about it? If someone were to stimulate his cerebellum, he wouldn't feel anything. There must be some fundamental difference between the cerebrum and cerebellum that causes us to call one conscious and the other not conscious. The answer became clearer to Jonah as he watched the whale swim around completely oblivious to Jonah's thoughts. The difference between the cerebellum and the cerebrum was the same as the difference between Jonah and the whale. Jonah was conscious but could not communicate this to the whale. If one would ask the whale if it were conscious of Jonah's thoughts the whale would say "no." Yet Jonah was conscious. If one would ask the whale if it were conscious of its own cerebellar function the whale would say "no." Yet the cerebellum was conscious, perhaps in a different way or at a different level of complexity than other brain areas, but nonetheless conscious. Jonah then considered that there then may be no fundamental difference in what we call "conscious" and "unconscious," except insofar as the former is *communicable by the person to others*, whereas the latter is not communicable. Jonah imagined, for instance, a situation in which a person was shown a picture of a tree and then asked to raise his hand when he became aware of the picture. Circuitries in the person's brain fired in a particular spatiotemporal pattern that corresponded to the awareness of "tree." If this occurred *and* the person raised his hand, then he was conscious of tree. If the circuitries fired and the person could not raise his hand or otherwise give any evidence of recognition of the tree, then there was *still* a consciousness of "tree" although many people might mistakenly conclude that there was no such consciousness. The person himself might conclude that there was no consciousness of "tree" if the areas of his brain that weighed the matter and gave out the report to others never received the information about "tree." What we are used to calling "conscious" is simply that form of consciousness that we can tell others about. The so-called "unconscious" is consciousness that we cannot tell others about.

A poisonous fish suddenly entered the whale's stomach and stung Jonah, paralyzing him temporarily. Jonah was unable to express anything to the outside world. He was conscious, though, just unable to express himself. What an anguish, trying to express himself but being unable to. Jonah wondered whether other, so-called unconscious areas of the body, experienced such an anguish. He speculated that this was not likely the case, because it would be unproductive from an evolutionary standpoint to have such an arrangement. Most likely, organs of the body proceed about their functioning in a conscious way without thinking "Help, let me out. I'm conscious and want to express myself." Most likely their level of complexity does not include such thoughts, in particular such a high level of complexity as to think in terms of "I."

Jonah did wonder, however, about what was termed the "unconscious mind". Perhaps it was not only conscious but at times does want to be let out and express itself, but is suppressed, leading, sometimes, to exacerbations of emotional or physical ills. During his paralysis, Jonah could not communicate his thoughts to the outside world, but he was still conscious, and so was his so-called "unconscious" mind. Both minds had difficulty communicating to the outside world. His so-called "unconscious" mind never gained the ability to communicate and people would continue to call it "unconscious" even though it really was conscious. His "conscious" mind recovered from the paralysis and people would say that Jonah was really conscious at the time of his paralysis because he later recovered and was able to tell about the experience. In reality, though, both "conscious" and "unconscious" minds were conscious (*).

---

*Jonah's new view of consciousness enables one to understand the results of what have been termed the "split-brain studies". Neurosurgeons, in rare cases of epilepsy, have found it helpful to sever all lines of communication between the right and left hemispheres of the brain. In that way, an epileptic seizure originating in one hemisphere will not spread to the opposite side. Studies on such patients produced striking evidence of independent functioning of the hemispheres. Normally, the left hemisphere controls speech function. A split-brain patient, when presented, through elaborate testing devices, with a picture of a spoon to the right hemisphere actually might *say* (using his left hemisphere) that he was unaware of any picture, but at the same time, the right hemisphere would direct the patient's hand to point out the spoon and clearly indicate its awareness of the spoon. Jonah's new view of consciousness enables one to understand this situation. Each hemisphere, whether in split-brain patients or in normal individuals, is associated with its own consciousness. The surgical splitting of the brain into two independently functioning hemispheres, each of which communicates separately with the outside world results in the appearance of two separate conscious entities. This should not be surprising as we normally have *many* conscious Jonahs inside of us (the cerebellum, liver, etc.), but since the body acts as a single functioning unit to communicate with the outside world, it appears to an observer (even to our-

Jonah was drawn to this line of reasoning although he could not *prove* that the argument was correct. He could not *prove* that the cerebellum was conscious. But then, he couldn't prove that anyone else except himself was conscious either. He had to allow himself the liberty of using at least a little *inductive reasoning* to reach such conclusions. Inductive reasoning is a form of logic that uses one's common experience to predict that events that occurred will occur again. For instance, if the sun has risen every day for centuries, inductive reasoning tells us that it will rise again. If we note that we look like other people in respect to our general outside shape, our internal anatomy, and our behavior, we presume that other aspects are similar, too, i.e., that if I am conscious, other people are conscious, too.

Inductive reasoning is far from conclusive. The proverbial chicken, which notes that it is being fed each day, inductively concludes that this feeding will continue forever — until the day the farmer kills it. Inductive reasoning can lead to wrong conclusions. One could be purist in reasoning and conclude only that "I think; therefore, I exist," but even this reasoning is faulty. Simply by saying "I think" presumes the existence of "I." Maybe there is no "I." Maybe it is true that "I think; therefore I don't exist," and our logic system is wrong. Jonah figured that if he were going to be that particular in his thinking he might as well anesthetize himself, lie down, and just die. Sure, he couldn't *prove* anything, but he was going to take his best crack at understanding reality by making a few minimal assumptions and using inductive reasoning in the process, despite its faults.

Jonah not only assumed that other people were conscious, but used his inductive reasoning in approaching the question of

---

selves!) that there is only one conscious mind. It should not be surprising to find two conscious entities associated with the same individual in the split brain studies. The appearance of two conscious entities occurs because the two hemispheres independently communicate with the outside world, rather than presenting themselves as a single functioning unit. (See Appendix I: The Meaning of "I").

individual organ consciousness. He reasoned that one part of the brain that was conscious resembled in its essential anatomical and physiological features other areas of the brain that previously were considered unconscious. By inductive reasoning he favored the interpretation of reality that held consciousness to exist in all parts of the brain, but perhaps in different degrees of complexity. Continuing further, why should neuronal tissue be conscious and nonneuronal tissue, such as the liver, be unconscious? They both contain cells that communicate in varying degrees with one another. Inductive reasoning again favored the view that consciousness was associated with both brain and nonbrain tissues, albeit perhaps in different degrees of complexity. Not every organ is so advanced as to think in terms of "I." Some of them, like the liver just go about doing their business consciously without ever thinking anything so complex as "I am a liver." Nonetheless, all the organs are conscious, only in different degrees of complexity. The difference between organs that were previously called "conscious" and "unconscious" would lie solely in the ability of the individual to *express to the outside world* the thought associated with the organ in question. All organs are conscious to different degrees, however elementary. Most do not express themselves outwardly.

Jonah then extended his inductive reasoning from humans to other animals. Why should human cells be associated with consciousness and not the cells of other animals? They are all cells. If there were a difference in this regard, one would have to explain why such a fundamental difference of having or not having consciousness should exist when cells appear so similar. As lower animals and plants all consist of cells, they should be conscious, too, although the level of complexity may be much less, and a human would have difficulty in comprehending what such low-level conscious experiences feel like.

Extending the inductive process further, Jonah reasoned that there are no clear cut criteria that distinguish living from nonliving. Life itself is a continuum that ranges from the most elementary rock to the most advanced life form (as in Jonah's dream of the two planets in Chapter 3). It is the same for consciousness. Inanimate objects consist of molecules just as do animate objects. The degree of molecular complexity changes as a continuum from the stone through the human. A stone could exhibit consciousness, too, although to such an elementary degree as to be incomprehensible by our minds, which must think at a higher level of organization.

Jonah summarized his thoughts: Everything in the universe is conscious, but perhaps in different degrees of complexity. In some cases, an individual can tell others about that conscious experience. In other cases, he cannot. We have been used to calling the former situation "conscious" and the latter situation "unconscious." However, in reality, all thoughts are conscious, but some of them cannot be expressed by the individual, just as Jonah's thoughts cannot be expressed by the whale. *There is more consciousness in the world than one might realize.*

Although still dreaming, Jonah slept again within his dream, this time dreaming a new dream within his original dream.

CHAPTER 5.

JONAH BECOMES A COMPUTER.

Are Computers Conscious?

In his dream, Jonah imagined his own brain of 14 billion nerve cells with their innumerable interconnections. (The brain performs many vital functions. Some involve the *reception* of incoming information, some the *integration* of that information, some the *storage* of that information, some the *transfer* of that information to other brain areas, or out of the brain to other areas.) A neurosurgeon was operating on Jonah's brain, replacing, one by one, each protoplasmic nerve connection with a fine metallic wire that would maintain the same brain functioning. With the first wire in place, Jonah felt no difference in his conscious experience. The brain was still functioning in the same way. As more and more connections were replaced with wires, Jonah still felt no change in his conscious experience. Soon all of Jonah's nervous system was replaced by metallic circuitry. He was, in effect, a highly advanced computer with all his previous memory associations and other brain functions still intact. Jonah still felt no change in his consciousness. His behavior was for all practical purposes the same.

This did not surprise Jonah, for the *information* content in his head was not changed; why, therefore, should he visualize a square instead of a circle on viewing a circle? The relations between all the elements of his past experience were unchanged, even though the vehicles for carrying that information (metallic wires versus protoplasm) were different. What difference should it make whether it were molecules of protoplasm or molecules of computer electronics that constituted the vehicle of information transfer and storage? The same musical selection can be stored on a tape or on a compact disc. It is the stored information, not the vehicle of storage, that is critical in identifying the particular piece of music.

Jonah looked at the lining of the whale's stomach, which he previously noted to be red like a cherry. It still looked red like a cherry to him. He could not, however, rule out the possibility that it actually was some other color. That is, his new metallic brain circuitries may have responded to his looking at the lining with the information that the color looked "the same as before the brain operation, the same as the color of cherries." He might, however, actually be having the conscious experience of green but still be concluding that what he was seeing was the same as before the operation. He would, however, be associating the new conscious experience (now green) with "the color of cherries," and think that this has always been the color of cherries. If he actually felt, "Hey, something's wrong; this looks green like grass now, not red like a cherry as I previously noted," then we would have to say that the information content of his circuitries had changed, that the brain now associated the color of the whale's stomach lining with the color of grass, whereas such an association never existed previously. But the new Jonah performed in the very way that the old Jonah performed. Jonah could actually have seen the stomach lining as the visual experience of green now, but all his other color associations would be changed in a matching way. Thus, the visual experience of green, to the new Jonah, would now be associated with the color of cherries, and the visual experience of red might be associated with the color of grass, but nothing would seem different. Regardless of whether the "red" he saw now was the same as the "red" he saw previously, Jonah postulated that at least the informational *associations* between the elements of his consciousness remained the same after the operation. If the *root* elements differed, i.e., if the basic perception of "red" or "green" had changed, it was not apparent to him and it made little difference. He was just as happy with his new computer-based functioning. As long as the informational associations remained the same, a person should notice no change in the conscious experience, regardless of the makeup of the vehicle for carrying that information, whether protoplasm or computer electronics. The human mind rebels against such a suggestion because of a persisting prejudice that imparts a mysterious vitalistic force to protoplasm. But does not protoplasm consist of molecules just as does any arrangement of computer electronics? Are certain molecules to be regarded as conscious, and others not? Surely, unless one maintains a vitalistic point of view, consciousness depends on interrelationships, not on the medium that provides the vehicle for such interrelationships.

Jonah had concluded that the activities of all parts of the brain, all parts of the body, all objects, whether protoplasmic or not, including computers, were associated with some level of conscious experience. Insofar as what those conscious experiences were, his experience with his operation, but also his *inductive reasoning* told him that if the informational *associations* in his brain circuitry firing patterns remained intact, then his conscious experiences would appear to remain the same to him after transformation from a human to a computer. It was the *informational content*, rather than the physical makeup of the circuitry that was critical to the quality of consciousness. He could not say for sure whether the actual green that he saw was the same as that of the computerized version, but this was an unimportant issue so far as how he felt. Everything seemed the same.

Jonah therefore considered two kinds of information content as being associated with consciousness. One he called *root* information, which included basic qualities, such as (perhaps) a particular color, smell, sound pitch, etc. The other kind of information was *associational* information, which included all the associations among root informations (e.g., green being associated with grass, red with cherries, etc.). He concluded that the associational information was identical in the old Jonah and the computerized Jonah, but he could not conclude whether the root information was duplicated. Indeed, he could not even form an opinion as to whether the color "red" that one person saw and reported was the same as the color red that some other person saw on looking at the same object.

Regardless of whether or not the "root" information remained the same, Jonah still thought that he felt the same as before. He felt that if he were to die, it would make little difference whether or not the root information remained the same; if associational information were to remain unchanged, he would be quite content. So long as the associational information remained the same he would feel that his consciousness remained unchanged. But why should information of any kind remain when he died? The brain would die, and wasn't the presence of all this information contingent on the existence of the brain?

With this discouraging thought, Jonah slept.

CHAPTER 6.

JONAH DREAMS OF A HORSE IN A WOODEN BLOCK.

Where Is Consciousness?

In this dream, Jonah contemplated a piece of black paper. But this was no ordinary paper. It once was a white piece of paper. A picture was drawn on that page, and then another and another, until the page eventually became so full that it appeared black. That black page was the sum total of all those pictures and actually contained far more information than one could suppose, in fact all the information in the universe.

Then a solid block of wood appeared before Jonah. A sculptor carved out a beautiful bust of a horse. But was the horse not inside the block before the sculptor arrived? The sculptor simply freed it from its case. That block contained all the possible sculptures in the universe, including a sculpture of Jonah's brain and its circuitries. Every moment that went by, one could imagine within the block a different sculpture of the changing circuitry patterns in Jonah's brain, patterns that duplicated in sculptured form the information in his brain, duplicating his consciousness. Did one need a brain for a conscious experience to exist? Did not all of consciousness exist in all of matter in any part of the universe?

Then a hologram appeared before Jonah, a light image fixed in space of Jonah's brain with all its circuitries, changing in time in a fashion that duplicated the spatiotemporal changes in his real thinking brain. This too duplicated the associational information content of his brain, the essence of consciousness. Did one in fact need matter for consciousness to exist?

Then all these images disappeared and Jonah was left staring into blank space. This, too, duplicated his consciousness, as blank space could be considered to be divided into potential points, points that could duplicate any geometric relationships that one wished. Such points could duplicate the associational relationships of the circuitry patterns in Jonah's brain, i.e., duplicate the associational information in Jonah's brain, duplicate his consciousness. It was not the nature of the materials that carried the information that mattered; it was the information itself, the relationships. If the informational associations were duplicated, the conscious associations were duplicated. Infinite consciousness could exist in a vacuum. Such consciousness might not be able to accomplish anything in the real universe, but it nonetheless existed.

Jonah extrapolated his thoughts to all areas of the universe: Information was everywhere, and consciousness, including his own consciousness, was associated with everything in every area of the universe. It was not only his present consciousness, but all his past and future consciousness, all his potential consciousness, that existed everywhere—and this did not depend on the existence of his body.

Jonah summarized his thoughts: Consciousness need not be associated only with particular areas of the brain. It is associated with all areas of the brain. What we have been used to calling the "unconscious" mind is simply a conscious mind, a Jonah-in-the-whale, which cannot communicate its consciousness to the centers that tell the outside world about it.

Consciousness is not confined to the nervous system, either. It may be associated with non-nervous tissues, with non-human life forms, in fact, with computers, the complexity of consciousness depending upon the complexity of the information processing. A computer whose circuitry contained the same informational relations as Jonah's brain, although made of different materials and using a different informational coding system, had similar associational consciousness, although Jonah could not be sure about whether the computer had the same root conscious experiences. It was the similar informational *as-*

sociations in the computer circuitries and Jonah's brain that accounted for the similarity in consciousness between the computer-brain and Jonah. Infinite information potentially exists at every point in the universe. Thus, Jonah's consciousness existed everywhere, and was not dependent on the existence of his body. Then what did the brain do, and why do we say that consciousness is dependent on the brain and disappears with the loss of the brain? We have been used to saying that consciousness disappears when the brain disappears because there is no longer a brain to communicate to the outside world its experience of consciousness. But consciousness is always there, even if there is no brain. Consciousness pre-exists, because infinite information pre-exists. The brain duplicates and reveals items of consciousness that pre-exist in the infinite consciousness that permeates the universe: Just as a sculptor removes, or frames, the bust of the horse from the block of wood, within which the bust of the horse pre-exists, so does the brain. The informational content of the brain is like the horse. It exists everywhere in its potential form. The brain brings it into this world in an active form. Each conscious experience arises from a block of preexisting infinite consciousness within which the particular conscious experience resides.

Jonah was happy with the possibility that his consciousness might persist despite his death, but did not wish to be drawn into such a favorable conclusion simply because he wished the results to come out that way. As he recalled from his old Latin class, *"Semper credimus quod volumus"* ("We often believe that which we wish to believe"). There was more to be clarified: What was "information", and what was it about a particular circuit pattern that associated it with the conscious experience of "green", or the taste of "coffee"?

And Jonah slept.

CHAPTER 7.

JONAH TRIES TO SETTLE AN ISSUE BETWEEN TWO FEUDING COMPUTER DISKETTES.

Consciousness as Information.

In this dream, Jonah saw two computer diskettes. One was an exact copy of the other. A dispute broke out between the diskettes as to what constituted their true information content. It would appear that they ought to contain the same information, as they were duplicates. The only problem was that diskette A, when booted up on computer A, gave a screen readout of the word "NO," whereas diskette B, when booted up on computer B, gave a readout of "YES." How could this be?

The answer lay in the differing hardware of computer A and computer B. Computer A was set up to interpret either diskette as "NO," whereas computer B was set up to interpret either diskette as "YES." Did the two diskettes contain the same information?

The answer, Jonah realized, had to be formulated within the context in which the diskettes were used. In relation to computer A, the diskettes carried the information "NO"; and in relation to computer B the diskettes carried the information "YES." Jonah tried to resolve the dispute. He did not feel it was appropriate to tell the diskettes that neither of them carried any information. After all, they had a price tag of $78.00 in the computer store. They had something on them, and he could not just tell them that they had no information content. It also seemed inappropriate to say arbitrarily that a particular diskette carried a "YES" or a "NO." He concluded that the best resolution of the problem was to say that they contained both the information "YES" and "NO," either of which could be expressed, depending on which computer was used. Similarly, the sound "HEE" means "he" in

English but "she" in Hebrew. Rather than say that the sound has no meaning, one may say it carries the potential of meaning "he" or "she," depending on the interpreter. Jonah made the diskettes feel really good by informing them that they each contained infinite information, as all kinds of screen readouts could be obtained if one imagined infinite varieties of computers, each interpreting the same diskette differently. The information on the diskettes was in symbolic form. What the symbols stood for could be anything, depending on how the code was interpreted by differing computers. Each diskette contained not only infinite information, but also infinite consciousness, consciousness being associated with information.

Just then, a tree fell in a forest. Jonah saw it fall, but, being inside a sealed room, heard nothing. Did the tree make a sound? Certainly Jonah could not say it made a sound of a particular pitch, for, clearly, an observer standing nearby would hear a different pitch than an observer rapidly traveling toward or away from the tree (just as you hear a higher pitch when a car speeds toward you than when the car speeds away from you). So, if one were to say that a sound of a given pitch really occurred, one would also have to say that many other pitches occurred, too, to correspond to the potential sounds heard by many different observers traveling at different speeds in relation to the tree. One would have to go beyond that, as well. Imagine that someone hooked one's optic nerve to one's auditory nerve in such way that a sound wave would end up stimulating the visual area of the brain. In such a case the falling tree would produce a sound in respect to the normal observer but a visual perception in respect to the operated observer.(*) In fact, one would have to say that the tree's falling not only correlated with

---

*Neurosurgical procedures involving the electrical stimulation of various areas of the brain have demonstrated on numerous occasions that the particular kind of perception reported by a patient depends on the area of the brain that is stimulated. A visual perception results from stimulating the visual area, an auditory perception from stimulating the auditory area, etc.

sounds and visual impressions but every kind of conscious experience, depending on the interpreting system, the interpreting system being different brain areas in this case rather than different computers. We can picture an imaginary interpreting system in the air responding to the tree falling and reponding with any number of patterns that would correspond to all sorts of conscious information patterns. The particular associational information pattern in the interpreting system would correspond to a particular conscious experience.

An observer entered the forest and looked at a tree. The flashing shuttles of interweaving patterns in his brain circuitries then carried the information of a tree and corresponded to the conscious image of the tree. But what about the actual tree? Did it in itself (i.e., in respect to itself alone) contain the same information about "tree" as did the circuitry patterns in the observer's brain? Not quite. For one thing, the observer saw only one view of the tree. The actual tree contained *more* information than that one view: information about it from another angle, information about its submicroscopic structure, etc. Moreover, in another sense, the actual tree contained *less* information than that associated with the observer's brain circuitries. The information in the observer's circuits consisted not only of the incoming information about the tree but had added to it other information from the observer's brain. For instance, the observer may have liked trees, and the picture of the tree that he had may have had the additional information that told him that the image was a favorable one. Moreover, the observer used his eyes to see the tree, and the information of "used my eyes; vision" was also tacked onto the information. Additionally, in the development of the nervous system from the embryo, undoubtedly there is much information built into the nervous system on a genetic basis that is quite apart from any environmental influences. The child is born with sucking and grasp reflexes, the ability to respond to pain, etc. How much of the information that pertained to the observer's conscious impression of the tree was derived from the environment, and how much previously existed in the brain? There undoubtedly was some information, and hence consciousness, about "tree" that was inherent in the tree itself; but that information was in some ways less and in some ways more than that experienced by the observer.

As the observer was leaving the forest, an arrow flew through the air, striking him in the brain. This focal trauma stimulated the visual area of the brain in such a way that it produced the visual impression of a tree. Such events are known to neurosurgeons, who have often noted that detailed and duplicatable conscious experiences can be generated by stimulating certain regions of the brain. Did the arrow contain the information about the tree? In relation to the brain area it did, but one really could not at all make a case to say that the arrow, independent of the brain, carried the information for tree. Similarly the computer diskettes, by themselves did not carry information for "yes" or "no" unless they were thought of in the context of the interpreting system (the computer). Information proved to be an elusive entity, depending on the context of the interpreting system to which the object in question was subjected. Objects appear to have certain information intrinsic to themselves, but have far more information when thought of in the context of any variety of different interpreting systems.

This left Jonah with the question about why the information content in his own brain should correspond to any particular conscious experience. The information in his brain could be symbolic for virtually anything. What was the interpreting system for the information in his own brain? Why should the information in the inherent firing pattern of his brain circuits come up with the visual impression of a "green leaf" or a particular sound?

CHAPTER 8.

JONAH TRIES TO ENVISION A CONSCIOUS QUARK.

When Did Consciousness First Arise in the Universe?
What Occurred During Creation?

Jonah's dream shifted to another scene. Physicists throughout the world were trying to unify the universe through a single grand, but simple, equation that accounted for all the forces in nature. They had an intuitive feeling that this approach was warranted, and their efforts were spurred by continuing successes in developing simplified formulae that accounted for diverse phenomena: Electricity and magnetism became describable as a single phenomenon — electromagnetism. Time and space became fused in relativity theory as a four-dimensional time-space continuum. Matter and energy became interchangeable. The diversity of types of matter long ago had become simplified by the discovery that the innumerable kinds of molecules all turned out to be composed of some 100 or so kinds of atoms in the periodic table. Each of the 100 kinds of atoms was composed of protons, neutrons, and electrons. There were even further simplifications in the schemata in that protons and neutrons, and many other kinds of subatomic particles, were found to consist of simpler units called "quarks" and "leptons." There was every indication that everything was heading toward some kind of grand unification theory in which a very simple mathematical formula would describe everything in the universe. The primary stuff of the universe would not be a *multitude* of entities but very few or even a single entity, a sort of quark, from which would stem, by appropriate combinations with itself (or themselves), the full range of diversity that constitutes the universe. The universe would then have a very simple origin in the form of a building block from which everything was constructed.

There was another issue, however, that didn't seem to get much recognition, but was just as important: the origin of consciousness. How was it that "red," "coffee taste," the sound of the note "C sharp," the smell of a "rose", the feeling of "love" came to be? Some people dismissed this as a much later development in the evolution of the universe, as if consciousness per se did not arise until living things reached a certain level of complexity. Jonah, however, knew otherwise. Consciousness was not the product of complexity (although there may be certain degrees of complexity of consciousness). It was not restricted to humans or even to protoplasm. It existed in conjunction with everything in the universe and must have arisen along with everything else in the universe. If one could account for the creation of matter, how could one account for the creation of a conscious feeling?

Jonah considered the question of the smallest division of a conscious feeling. For instance, the conscious feeling of a "green leaf" could be divided into "green" and "leaf." There was an *association* between "green" and "leaf." "Leaf", itself could be subdivided into other associations, like "the shape of the leaf," "the veins of the leaf," the "cells of the leaf," etc. But what about the color "green"? Was "green" the smallest subdivision of itself? Was it a root element in the sphere of consciousness? If so, then one would have to acknowledge that consciousness has many root subdivisions, for one would have to contend not only with other colors, but with taste, smell, sound, and touch, among other conscious feelings. The same intuition that led scientists to question whether matter had a simple root led Jonah to ask whether "green" could itself be subdivided.

At first Jonah tried to subdivide "green" into "vision, the eyes" and "green devoid of vision," but he had difficulty with this. Was "green" a true root or was it just that the human brain lacked the ability to subdivide "green" further? To one person, a note sounded on a trumpet may appear to be a true root, whereas another person may be able to recognize the sound as not being truly pure and break it down into several subcomponents.

Jonah considered that if one really felt intuitively about a simple primary event in the formation of the universe, one had to include consciousness in that formulation. If one included consciousness and the formulation was still going to be simple, then consciousness itself had to have simple root elements, which by their various combinations with one another (just as combinations of certain quarks form a proton) would form higher order conscious experiences, such as a particular color, smell, or taste, etc. What that original "conscious quark" was like was totally incomprehensible to Jonah. Perhaps he saw "green," but could not recognize the subdivisions, just as a person could see a building from afar but not recognize the bricks that composed the building. The combinations of conscious quarks in his brain formed a composite picture (equivalent to the bricks forming a house), and it was only the composite picture that he could *describe to others*. Thus, although there was associated with his brain individual conscious quarks, only the composite of many quarks could be expressed to others. Thus "green" is what we feel and can express to others, whereas the quark, although a conscious quark, is delegated to what customarily is called the unconscious mind.

Jonah went a step further. He questioned whether or not point-like quarks were even necessary in the above scheme of things. In other words, it makes little difference, in the appearance of a house, when seen from afar, whether it is made of stone or plastic bricks. It is the *association* of the bricks, regardless of the bricks' makeup, that makes the house. What difference would it make what the makeup was of the bricks (quarks) if the associations between them were still those of a house (or a green leaf in this case)? Perhaps the associational aspect was all that was necessary for the conscious experience. What those associational relationships were remained completely incomprehensible to Jonah, for he could not even subdivide "green."

What, indeed, if there were no point-like quark? Jonah imagined mathematically proscribed relationships between blank spaces, associational relationships that duplicated the quark relationships. Just as he had originally concluded (see section on The Horse In the Block) that consciousness (if defined in terms of relationships) could exist even in a vacuum, perhaps, then, no quarks would be needed. Any root of consciousness would not be some quark-like *point* of consciousness but an elementary conscious root *relationship* that could exist even in a vacuum. All of the potential conscious experiences would be built up from this elementary root relationship (one could call this relationship a "quark" if one wanted, but one must bear in mind that now one is talking not about a pointlike something but about a relationship).

Extending his thoughts further, Jonah considered whether it was necessary to postulate quarks for both matter and consciousness, resulting in a world of both mind and matter. Perhaps only one kind of quark was necessary. The original creation of the world need only have consisted of the creation of the primary conscious quark (or quarks), which by combination with itself (or themselves) produced all the varieties of conscious experience, including not only sight, sound, touch, smell, and taste, but matter, time, and space. After all, is it not true that the only thing that a person can experience in his life is his own consciousness? We presume that there is an outside world, and indeed, that outside world may even exist, but perhaps that world consists of consciousness and is made of the same materials as is our own consciousness. It would be sort of like a person having a dream in which he dreams of himself having a dream. The outside world would be a dream, and a person's perception of that outside world would constitute a dream within a dream. That dream within a dream would be made of the same stuff as the original outside world. If the outside world is just consciousness, then there would be no need to postulate the existence of both mind and matter. Mind and matter would be the same thing. To Jonah this was a relatively simple hypothesis, simpler than the supposition that mind and matter exist as separate entities.

Jonah postulated the primary event in the formation of the universe as the creation of a conscious quark(s) which by various combinations with itself (or themselves) produced matter, space, time, and every variety of conscious experience. There was nothing in his experience to suggest that the outside world consisted of anything other than consciousness itself. The only things that he or anyone else on earth had ever been aware of were conscious experiences. What evidence was there for the existence of anything else but consciousness? Included in this conscious universe were brains (made of consciousness) that, by the pattern of firing of their neurons, mathematically duplicated, in encoded form, the patterns of conscious quark combinations that corresponded to, in fact were, conscious feelings. What occurred in thinking of a "green leaf" was that associational patterns of neuronal firing within the brain duplicated the associational patterns of quarks that corresponded to "green leaf." When bricks form a house, the physical composition of the bricks makes little difference to the idea of "house." There is still the "house," regardless of whether the bricks are stone or plastic; it is the pattern of arrangement of the bricks that make the idea of "house." Similarly, a conscious experience of "house" depends not on physical composition of the brain but on the pattern of firing in the brain, the information carried by the brain. That pattern, and hence the conscious experience, is the product of numerous associational relationships built up at succeedingly higher hierarchical levels from the primary quark relationship.

Jonah then speculated about the creation of the universe. At first there was nothing. By nothing, there was really NOTHING, not only no matter, but also no time, space, or consciousness. Nothing means zero. Zero = 1-1, or 2-2, or infinity minus infinity. The presence of zero can be defined in terms of something minus itself. Something minus itself could exist when nothing existed. That was the formula for the creation of the universe: $0 =$ infinity minus infinity. Included within that infinity was the grand equation for the present universe. The equation reflected quark-like relationships that constituted space, time, matter, energy, and other forms of consciousness, all different expressions of conscious quark-like relationships. When the human brain became conscious of a "green leaf," what occurred was the duplication within the brain circuitry of the associative relationships that constituted the conscious experience of "green leaf".

If all that are necessary for the conscious experience are the *relationships* and not the point-like quark, then consciousness arises not as a by-product of the information in the patterned relationships of neuronal firing, but is *defined* by those relationships. It is extraordinarily difficult to picture how a given pattern of neuronal impulses can be *equivalent* to a particular conscious feeling, but this difficulty is to be expected because we have difficulty separating out the information from the *carrier* of that information. If we think of the neuronal firing pattern, we start to think of neurons, and electrophysiological discharges. The latter are not the information, but the carriers of that information. The information could be expressed in many ways, the electrophysiological firing pattern being just one way. If we start to think of the pattern strictly in terms of mathematical relationships, we start to think of the symbols used in mathematics, and the symbols are something else again, as contrasted with the associations, themselves. If a piece of music is recorded on a record, a tape, or a compact disc, we would say that each of these media contain the same information. We would not say that a primary part of the information is a round disc with grooves, or a floppy thin tape with electric charges. The latter carry the information, but do not constitute the information. Similarly, brain cells and their protoplasmic connections and electric discharges are not the information in the brain, but carry the information. The information devoid of the vehicle that carries it is the conscious experience(*). (See Appendix II: The Computer That Opted For Dualism).

Thinking along these lines presented certain advantages to Jonah. It simplified matters (or matter) by needing only one element (consciousness) in the world, rather than postulating two (consciousness and matter). This simplification was consistent with his experience of only being aware of his own conscious experiences: i.e., he had evidence of his own consciousness, but not necessarily of a separate outside world that was made of anything else but consciousness.

If it seemed difficult to imagine the creation of matter from nothing, it was easier to imagine the creation of a dream, at least a potential dream, from nothing. If nothing existed, the potential of an idea, the potential of a dream, at least the potential of a dream minus itself was easier to picture. This simplified the explanation of creation. Creation arose from zero. A potentiality could constitute a reality. The sculpture of a horse could exist in an uncarved block. And infinite consciousness existed everywhere. Jonah pictured the creation of a dream universe in which all potential conscious experiences (root consciousness experiences and all their potential associations into higher hierarchical order conscious experiences) arose from a single quark of consciousness. *Consciousness is information, and information is the set of associations among quarks of consciousness.*

Jonah stopped to view the patterns of firing within the whale's brain, as the whale contemplated the delicious smell of a field of krill food. Somewhere in the complex tangled circuitries of the whale's brain there was a firing pattern that corre-

---

*This is not to say that the information on the *record* is equivalent to the actual feeling of the music. The actual conscious feeling of the music is the combination of the information on the record plus additional information from our brains that is added on when listening to the record.

sponded to the smell of krill. But could not that pattern of firing in itself correspond to any number of codes for other patterns which would correspond to innumerable other conscious experiences? Why should we expect the whale's particular pattern of circuit firing to be associated with only one conscious experience? Why shouldn't it be associated with an infinite number of conscious experiences? Similarly, the pattern in Jonah's brain could be a code for many other kinds of patterns. The U.S. Bill of Rights, for instance, could be read as the Communist Manifesto if one used a particular coding system that translated one into the other. Couldn't the whale brain's firing pattern be a code for, be a symbol for, some other pattern that corresponded to some different associational conscious experience? Jonah thought about this and concluded that this was actually true. Anything going on in his own circuitries or the whale's circuitries corresponded to an infinity of conscious experiences, but the physical brain recorded and described to others only one pattern, one which had particular associations. A square may be used as a symbol for a triangle, but still a square has only 4 sides. If the brain circuitries, on viewing a square, contain information that says, perhaps in equation form, "4 equal sides all perpendicular to one another," that conceivably could be *symbolic* for a triangle and might be associated with consciousness of a triangle. However, the person will not report a triangle; he will report "4 equal sides all perpendicular to one another", i.e., a square. The "real" conscious experience, the one that the individual will attest to, and even draw, is the square, because that is the image ("4 equal sides all perpendicular to one another") that the individual reports. If there is absolute meaning to an elementary quark-like conscious relationship, there is absolute meaning to the hierarchy of complex consciousness that arises from those quark-like building blocks. Although a particular firing of a brain circuit may potentially be coded for an infinite number of conscious experiences, the "real" consciousness, the *one* the brain can tell about to the outside world, has a particular absolute set of associations, the ones associated with the conscious experience of "square." The brain reports the associations that it processes, not the symbolic significance that those associations might have in an outside system unattached to the observer.

Jonah thus pictured the origin of infinite consciousness as the primary event of creation. Included within this was the equation with the rules for our particular universe. As evolution proceeded, there arose single-celled organisms, multicellular organisms, and finally higher organisms, with brains, all of these things arising as conscious ideas. The brain itself was a conscious idea and so was the information within it, like a dream within a dream.

In his thoughts thus far, Jonah defined consciousness in terms of information. But what about "energy"? What role did the concept of energy (the "ability to do work") have in relation to the definition of consciousness? Jonah considered that there is a relationship between consciousness and energy (the ability to do work). A stone resting on the ground has minimal potential energy, in relationship to the ground. However, once elevated to a high platform, the stone, through no efforts of its own, suddenly acquires significant potential energy in relationship to the ground, even though it is still the same stone. Although elevated above the ground the stone may still be considered to have zero potential energy in relationship to the platform. Alternatively, the same stone may be regarded as having an enormous amount of potential energy in relation to some hypothetical non-existent object of great mass. It will not express such enormous potential energy in this world, though, as the object to which it is compared is only hypothetical. One can declare as much potential energy as one wishes on behalf of the stone provided one specifies the object that the stone relates to. Similarly, the information in the computer diskettes A and B may be a "yes" or a "no" in relation to the different computer interpret-

The

ing systems, or the information may be infinite in relation to some other, hypothetical, interpreting system. Energy tends to dissipate with time, a process called *entropy*. And so does information; the letters in a sentence written in soup with alphabet noodles will in time become randomized. The reverse is unlikely to occur. Energy may be regarded as a form of information and as a form of consciousness.

CHAPTER 9.

JONAH CONVERSES WITH A GRANDMOTHER CELL.

What is a Moment of Consciousness?

A television screen appeared before Jonah. The electrons moved across the screen with such great speed that the individual strike points were not perceptible. While Jonah did not see each electron strike the screen he did see the net effect, a picture of a lion spread across the monitor. Each electron did not contain the information of a lion but the net total picture did. What enabled Jonah to appreciate the picture as a whole was the rapid speed of the beam movement coupled with the brief period of persisting luminescence that allowed the complete picture to be visualized at once.

Jonah looked again at the screen. A new picture began to appear, only this time the raster movement was very slow, and the screen had no residual period of persisting luminescence. The only thing that Jonah saw was one dot at a time moving from spot to spot on the screen like a typewriter, but leaving behind no traces of the previous record. The picture that the television was supposed to create was the same lion, but it was imperceptible to Jonah. In order to appreciate the picture, Jonah had to picture the net total effect of the raster's excursions. If he considered what a *moment* of activity was like on the screen, it would not be anything resembling a lion. It would be a single meaningless dot. The net effect of *all* the electron beam's movements might carry the information of lion, but an isolated dot striking the screen at an isolated moment would not carry this information.

Jonah then asked himself if there was anything in our brains like a moment of consciousness. Do we not have a similar feature in our brain as does the TV screen? If we think of a lion, this involves many circuits firing over a small period of time. Suppose we slowed down that person's circuitries. Jonah visualized the person's thought processes slowing down, the speed of the person's conscious experiences slowing down, like a movie that was placed in slow motion. If we froze this firing to a particular moment, what would be the information content of the picture? Jonah imagined that it would not resemble a lion, but only a small section of the picture, unrecognizable as lion, as meaningless as the dot on the slowed-down TV screen. Perhaps, then, Jonah thought, when we think of our being conscious of something at a precise "moment," and picture a lion in a flash, we do not mean that we can actually experience a lion in a *moment*. Rather we mean that we experienced the picture over a small interval of time, which would be required to allow all of the lion circuitry to fire; *then* we can claim to have experienced a lion.

"Not so, sonny!" said a tiny voice within the visual area of the whale's brain. Jonah looked with surprise to determine the origin of this voice and saw a little cell shaped like an old woman in a rocking chair. "I am a grandmother cell," continued the old woman. "Neurophysiologists talk about me over coffee sometimes. It seems that complex information that enters the brain, in the visual system in my case, often converges to fire relatively few cells that ordinarily would not fire without that input. For instance, certain simple cells will not fire unless the incoming information is that of light shined on the retina. Other, more complex, cells will fire only if that information is that of a particular shape, for instance that of a line. More complex cells will not fire unless that particular line is moving in a particular direction. Take that same line and move it in a different direction and the cell will not fire. I am a grandmother cell. That means that I respond only to the specialized input of the picture of a grandmother. There are certain things the body will do if it sees a grandmother, like help it across the street. It won't do that unless the information of 'grandmother' registers in the brain. That information has to go through me. If I fire, then that is the equivalent to having seen a grandmother, and I relay that information along my nerve cell extensions in a chain that fires other neurons to help grandma across the street. If a neurosurgeon were to stimulate me with an electrode, the patient would report the vision of a grandmother. I feel I have a purpose in life, although to be strictly honest, there are some other grandmother cells, too, that help out. If I were to die, the brain would still function well, as it has the other grandmother cells to help out."

The grandmother cell continued: "The objection I have to your comparing the brain to a TV screen is as follows. For the TV screen, the information at any one moment is just that of the isolated dot on the screen. To get the overall picture of the lion, you have to put together the information from the overall dot pattern. In my case, however, all I have to do is fire. Just that act alone carries the information of 'grandmother', as I only fire in response to 'grandmother' input. What I influence after I fire is grandmother-related information. There is full information about grandmother just as I fire, whether or not that information came from seeing a grandmother or whether an electrophysiologist took a short cut and directly stimulated me with an electrode. I could not say that, however, about an isolated dot on the TV screen. My cell composition may to all superficial appearances resemble that of any other nerve cell, but the information that passes through is quite different. Not only is there consciousness of grandmother associated with my firing, but I can even describe this consciousness to others. But let's not talk about this right now. Why don't you just sit down and enjoy the show?"

"What show?" Jonah wondered, until he looked out and saw that the whale was approaching a rather fine specimen of female whale and making peculiar whale sounds that indicated that an act of mating was imminent. Certain actions of the male whale then transpired that led Jonah to conclude that the male had just experienced an orgasm. Jonah estimated the period of the whale's orgasm to be about 5 seconds.

"Not a bad guess," replied the grandmother cell, whose observation of the event was her main entertainment, since she was confined to a whale's brain. "It lasted exactly 5.5 seconds as measured on the whale's internal clock." The grandmother cell then showed Jonah a sort of organic clock within the confines of the whale's brain. "Without that internal clock, the whale would have significant difficulty in measuring time. We all have such a biological clock. Sure, even without the internal clock, one could always measure long periods of time according to how many moons transpired during an event. And for events shorter than a day, one could use a sundial, or, for more accurate measurements, a watch. However, say one were to speed up the sun or speed up one's wristwatch. Normally, in the presence of the internal clock, one would be able to tell that the sun and the watch were going faster than usual. Even if one speeded up all events outside the individual, one could tell that the events were speeded up. The internal clock enables one to make that determination. However, if one were to take away the internal clock, there would be real difficulty. Then, if one were to speed up all events outside the individual, including watches, one would have no idea that they were speeded up. In the absence of an internal clock, if one wished to check on how fast things were going by consulting an external clock, one would conclude that the (speeded up) events were going just as fast as ever, as the external clock was speeded up as well."

"It is the internal clock that gives us a sense of the speed of passing time. Picture all events in the universe, including all clocks *and* our body metabolism and our own internal clock, speeding up or slowing down and we wouldn't know the difference. We would have the same sense of time flowing at the same particular rate. If we were to speed up just this internal clock, we would have the sense that events that transpired took an awfully long time to occur, i.e., occurred rather slowly. If the clock were to be slowed to zero, we would have the sense that all events occurred instantaneously, that there was no time, that all events occurred" now, "with there being no such thing as a present or a past. What 'really' was the situation would depend on the observer of these events and the status of his clock."

"But what if there were no observer?" Jonah asked. "Time has no intrinsic meaning; it is relative," said the grandmother cell. "Time is simply what we measure on a clock, to paraphrase Einstein. We have this time sense because of our internal clock. This clock enables us to wake up at a particular time in the morning without using an alarm clock. Our bodies have certain intrinsic rhythms that constitute the clock, and we base our sense of the time of outside events in relation to the rhythm of this clock. Now watch this, sonny."

The old woman proceeded to speed up the whale's clock by a factor of 10. Where Jonah's clock would read the passage of 6 seconds, the whale's clock read the passage of 60 seconds. As these changes were being made, the whale came back for another pass at his mate. This time it experienced, in its own mind, a whale of an orgasm. The timing of the event seemed the same to Jonah, but from the whale's point of view, it lasted 10 times longer than before. The old woman then slowed down the whale's clock to one tenth its normal speed.

"Now watch this. Here he comes again," said the old woman. The whale, encouraged by his remarkable display of virility, made another attempt, and was in fact successful, but this time, although the elapsed time seemed the same to Jonah, from the whale's perspective, the event seemed to last far too short a time. The whale looked quite disappointed, which only confused his mate, who was quite satisfied with the outcome of events and congratulated her partner on the consistency of his performance.

The point that Jonah learned, apart from the entertainment interests of certain old women, was that his concept of time had a lot to do with the comparison of his internal clock with events of the outside world. One's conception of fast or slow had to relate to some standard with which to assess an event's time course. If one did not have an internal clock and simply relied on an external clock for measuring an event's time course, then one would have no way of feeling whether both event and external clock were going very fast or whether the event and the external clock were moving slowly. In order to actually feel the speed of time, an event has to be in relation to an internal clock. If the internal clock is altered, then the perception of the time course of events may be altered.

Jonah wondered what would happen if the whale were to view a picture of a grandmother. Could Jonah determine *the exact time* when the whale became conscious of the grandmother image? Such a picture was fortunately available, and as the whale viewed it, Jonah looked at the whale's internal clock, which was now back to running at exactly the same speed and time as Jonah's watch. Impulses sped down the whale's optic nerve carrying the grandmother information into the visual area of the whale's brain. The impulses converged on the grandmother cell, and from there went to the clock, which marked the time of grandmother visualization as precisely the moment the clock was struck. If one were to ask the whale exactly when it saw "grandmother," it would have given the time registered on the clock. Although consciousness of "grandmother" might have occurred earlier, i.e., while or prior to striking the grandmother cell (as the information for grandmother existed before the time that the grandmother cell was fired), the whale's actual report of the time of its consciousness coincided with the time of registering this information on the clock. The whale might say, for instance, "I was conscious of grandmother at precisely 4 seconds after 2," the time at which its clock received the information. Consciousness of "grandmother" really existed at *all* times and at all points in the universe (infinite consciousness being everywhere), but to the whale it was conscious of grandmother at precisely the time registered on its internal clock. When was it *really* conscious of grandmother—while the information was racing toward the grandmother cell, while the information fired the grandmother cell, or when the internal clock was being struck? Jonah concluded that the whale's consciousness of grandmother always existed, but the presence of the internal clock fooled the whale into thinking that that awareness had occurred at the particular time that the clock was struck.

Jonah imagined a functioning brain that gradually slowed in its physiologic functioning, like a movie run in slow motion. What would happen to conscious thought as time slowed? If it normally took several minutes to complete a sequence of neurophysiological firings that were associated with an event of consciousness (say a sequence of thinking about children, parents, grandfathers, grandmothers, and great-grandparents), and it now took several hours to complete the same sequence, Jonah pictured the simultaneous slowing of the conscious experience to coincide with the slowing of physiologic functioning.

And what if time were slowed to a dead halt, say at the point of thinking of grandmother? The point of thought that was frozen at that particular moment, (grandmother, in relationship to the total pattern of occurrences) would remain frozen as well. Of course with no activity occurring at all in the brain, one could imagine all kinds of combinations of circuitries that might have been firing at that time. But in relationship to the events that were occurring prior to the time of the freeze, and the events that those occurrences were heading for, the conscious experience of "grandmother" would remain frozen (even if there were no individual "grandmother" cells).

Jonah next imagined events in the brain occurring at their normal speed, but communication occurring not along fixed protoplasmic connections, but along electromagnetic waves. I.e., diverse parts of the brain were separated from each other by many miles and communicated among themselves by electromagnetic waves. What would happen to consciousness then?

Following his preceding line of reasoning, Jonah concluded that consciousness would still persist as before. The communication, the interrelationships in the flow of information remained the same, and consciousness would remain the same.

Jonah had concluded that consciousness persisted after death as infinite information always exists and the presence of information implied the existence of consciousness, including his own consciousness. But what of his "real" consciousness, the consciousness he could describe to others in this world? What would happen to that after death? Was there no longer any potential for it to communicate with the present world? Was it forever to remain in only a hidden potential form, incapable of participating in events in the present world? Jonah concluded that there is a form of such persistence. Everything that one does in this world leaves behind its influence in some chain of reactions that influences events far into the future. This influence is a form of information. It may be scattered diversely, remaining unassociated with any single body, but it is reflective of the very makeup of the individual that produced this ripple in the world. This influence, although scattered, is a form of consciousness. Just as one's conscious mind could remain unified despite separation of its elements across far distances, this influence that the individual has left upon the world remains as a unified expression of that person, a persisting consciousness that has real influence on the world even after an individual's death.

CHAPTER 10.

JONAH PICTURES FLATLAND.

Is It Possible to Picture a Fourth Dimension or Have a New Kind of Conscious Experience? How Much Can One Be Conscious of at Once?

Jonah tried to imagine the difficulties that someone trapped in a two dimensional world would have in picturing a world of three dimensions. Was it conceivable that such an inhabitant of Flatland could picture a three-dimensional world? Could not the information for three dimensions be ingrained in his two-dimensional brain in some mathematical formulation that contained the three-dimensional information in encoded form? Jonah concluded that such a possibility existed.

It was also in principle possible for a person in a three-dimensional world to comprehend a four-dimensional or higher world. The problem was that in practice neither the inhabitant of Flatland nor the inhabitant of our present world ever experienced the actual world of a higher dimension. Simply presenting an equation for a straight line ($mx + b = y$) is insufficient to allow a visualization of a straight line, unless one already has a picture of what an x and y axis are in space. The information for an axial system is not automatically ingrained in that equation; the x and y could stand for anything, not just two axial lines that are perpendicular to one another. The input from the actual environment provides the additional information, albeit in encoded form. Such encoded information could be inscribed into the brain of the Flatland inhabitant, and he too could be able to visualize a higher dimensional world. It is just that environmental conditions never allowed the impression of that information. In our world, it is also conceivable that we could envision higher dimensions. It is just that the environmental information for that has not reached our brains. And present mathematical formulae that describe the higher dimensions in abstract form, while helping somewhat in predicting certain features of that higher dimension, are insufficient (as in the case of mx + b = y) to fully describe that world in a way that is easily visualised. An equation that uses more than three axes, leaves out the *visualization* of the four-dimensional space in which those axes fit. Conceivably, though, the actual information of visualization of such space could be placed in encoded form, and experienced.

Jonah wondered whether it was possible to have a conscious experience of a totally different color or have some other experience apart from those normally experienced by people. Just as a blind person has difficulty in understanding what vision is, perhaps there are kinds of conscious experiences that we have never experienced but which are potentially possible. Dogs can hear pitches higher than we can. Bats and dolphins, which can navigate by sonar, may have a different sort of perception than humans have. It is conceivable that a new conscious experience could be achieved through our brains, but the existent wiring is not set up to fire along those lines (except possibly to some degree in certain conditions of altered mental states). It is conceivable that in principle, added wiring to our own brains, or alterations in the present wiring, could give rise to new types of conscious experiences.

How much can one be conscious of at once? What are the difficulties in conceiving of everything in the universe at once? We might expect that by thinking "everything" we are actually using this code word to think about all that there is. However, just thinking "everything" does not enable one to contemplate everything. For one thing, we do not have the knowledge in our brains to think of everything. Even if we were to study for many generations and gradually acquire all the information that our senses could conceivably acquire, that information would still be limited to the capacity of our senses. If there are other types of conscious experiences that human sense organs cannot detect (e.g., whatever the experience of sonar detection is to a bat or dolphin), then those experiences would be left out of such a world view, and the view of "everything" would be deficient. Moreover, even if all such conscious experiences could be acquired, there would be considerable difficulties in contemplating them as a whole within a short time. Say one had all the information that constituted "everything." If a person with all this information tried to contemplate everything, he could not immediately call to mind all these things that "everything" referred to in a way that *could be described to others* in a brief time. Our "real" consciousness, that which we can describe to others, takes time to reveal. We could not conceive and relate "everything" within a few minutes time, even if our brains had that stored information, as it would be impossible to go through all that mass of information in a relatable manner in just a few minutes. We could spill out a few of the things that "everything" refers to, but not all of them. We could act with great efficiency to think of as many things as possible, in an organized manner, within a short time. But we could not perceive everything. However, if we do not limit our definition of consciousness to describable conscious experiences, then the consciousness of everything in the universe is everywhere, including our own brains, at all times. Only a small part of it, however, can be described and brought into the world.

PART II.
GOD

Chapter 11.

JONAH THINKS ABOUT GOD

As Jonah sat within the whale's bowels, he recognized his great danger and poor prognosis. As often occurs to people under adverse circumstances, thoughts of "God" arose in Jonah's mind. Was there a God, and if so, could God help him? From whence does there arise in a person the concept of "God"?

Jonah returned to the image of the arrow that flew through the air. It had struck a person right in the visual area of the brain and therein, by direct visual stimulation of the brain, called forth the visual perception of a tree. Was it correct to say that that arrow contained the information for tree? If one were to actually come across a tree and the light rays reflected from that tree were to strike the eye and be relayed to the brain as visual input, we would be more inclined to say that the light waves independently carried information about tree. But in the case of the arrow, no independent analysis of the arrow out of the context of the area struck by it could extract "tree" information. The light waves on the other hand could, by the analysis of its angles, produce the geometry of a tree, and one may say that it carried "tree" information. However, in order to extract this information about "tree" from the light rays, we have to use our brains. Who is to say that the situation of our analyzing these waves does not involve stimulation of brain areas in the same way as the arrow? Perhaps the perception of "tree" arises because our brain patterns are set up in such a way as to distort the information in some way, to add or detract from the information in some way as to produce something different? Certainly this is true to some degree, in that the information of "visual" is attached to the incoming information and there is nothing about the incoming light waves, before they reach the individual, that intrinsically carries the information of "visual."

Our brains are the product of millions of years of evolution. Even prior to any input from the outside environment, the brain is wired in complex ways. How much of our conscious experience truly reflects the outside world? How much reflects information that is inherited, the product of years of evolution, information that arises internally, much as the arrow that struck the brain simply triggers information that is already there? When one perceives of "God," to what degree, then, do such feelings arise from the integration of many environmental experiences, and to what extent do they arise from internal, preset wirings of the genome? Does God exist? If so, what was God, and could God help Jonah?

CHAPTER 12.

JONAH'S DESPAIR AND HIS QUANTUM EXPERIMENT.

Is There Free Will? Is There God? If There is a God,
Can God Influence the World?

Jonah saw no escape from the whale. The whale's digestive acids were beginning to affect him, and he saw only a painful death ahead. He contemplated doing away with himself. No one could help him. He could not help himself. Indeed, perhaps all his thoughts to date, all his previous concerns about his purpose in the world, were irrelevant because this was a deterministic world. Were not all events in the present universe predetermined eons ago through a chain of cause and effect? What difference would it make what he did? It would have been predetermined. Perhaps he should end it all now through drowning. Yet he could not make the decision.

Jonah closed his eyes. He saw himself propelled through outer space. There loomed before him a giant cubical, closed racquetball court, floating deep in space. Thousands of racquet balls were bouncing off the interior walls in an apparently random manner. These events had been occurring continuously for many centuries. At a particular time on Jonah's stopwatch there was a greater number of balls striking the left hand wall than the right. What had determined the imbalance of strikes at that particular moment?

Jonah looked back a few seconds in time and observed the balls. He had little difficulty in predicting what would be the outcome a few seconds later. In dealing with such a macroscopic event, involving large balls, it was easy to predict pretty accurately a few seconds into the future, provided he knew all the theoretically possible information about those balls. He could determine that there would be this imbalance of strikes simply by looking back at the situation a few seconds earlier. He found that he could go back even farther in time and make the prediction, but the farther back he went, the *less certain* he could be in the result. It was a strange state of affairs. Even if he were given all the theoretically possible information about each ball, he could not predict with absolute certainty the final behavior of the balls far into the future. If he predicted only a few seconds into the future, the predictions were virtually 100% accurate in a large number of trials. But if he tried to predict thousands of years in advance, the predictions became less reliable, even though he had all the theoretically possible information about the original state of the balls.

Then the court and the racquet balls became smaller, approaching the size of atoms. Jonah then found a change in the predictability of the strikes. Even going back a few seconds in time, it was difficult to predict with much certainty where the balance of hits would lie. The smaller the size of the balls, the less certain their behavior. Jonah did not exist in a deterministic universe but in a probablistic universe (*).

These findings gave Jonah momentary pause in his consideration of suicide. Perhaps there was meaning to the world after all. Perhaps he did have some say in the outcome of events. Perhaps events that occurred did not occur solely on a prede-

---

*The analogy here is with subatomic particles, which according to current physics (the "uncertainty principle" of quantum mechanics), behave in a probablistic way rather than in a deterministic manner. The uncertainty in a particle's behavior lies not in hidden variables that distinguish one particle from one another or in mechanical difficulties in obtaining precise measurements. Rather, the uncertainty is intrinsic to quantum mechanics, in which it is impossible to simultaneously know a particle's precise location and velocity, even given all the theoretically possible information about the particle. The smaller the particle, the greater the uncertainty. See Appendix III for further details of the relationship of consciousness to quantum mechanics. For reviews, see Wolf, Fred A., *Taking the Quantum Leap*, Harper and Row (1981); Pagels, Heinz R., *The Cosmic Code*, Simon and Schuster (1982).

termined basis. Perhaps there was free will. Free will could not exist in a deterministic universe. The finding of a non-deterministic universe, while not proving the existence of free will, did allow for its possible existence. The basis for free will, however, would have to lie in *microscopic* events within the processing of neuronal messages. Macroscopic events (as in the case of the real-life racquet balls) would be too predictable. The numerous uncertainties in the behavior of the atoms of a large object would largely balance each other out; it would require too long a time for the net accretion of uncertainties to amount to anything significant. Human free will decisions need to occur within a short time span. Microscopic events, e.g., at the chemical level of nerve firing, could be accompanied by sufficient uncertainties (i.e., whether or not the nerve cell should fire) as to allow a significant degree of uncertainty in the outcome of a cell's firing. The outcome would be particularly significant for the case of grandmother cells.

Jonah, though, realized these thoughts were pure speculation so far as free will is concerned. Just because an event is indeterminate, and can only be predicted on a probablistic basis, does not mean that the outcome is directed by any free will. The outcome may simply be based on random factors built into the mathematical grand equation of the universe. One could predict only on a probablistic basis which wall would receive the greater number of hits. If 50% of the time the balls would hit mainly the right hand wall and 50% of the time the left, then so far as Jonah could see, the decision one way or the other on a single given trial was purely random. Why postulate that some intervening "free will" determined the outcome of a particular trial?

Jonah reviewed the coincidences that had occurred while he was on ship —the storm, the drawing of straws. Were all these just random occurrences with nothing special underlying them? After all, unusual occurrences are bound to occur sometimes. Or was something else operating, the equivalent of free will, but on a higher plane? Did something direct the course of events, allow, on rare occasions, strange coincidences to occur, but within the allowances of probability in physics? Did Jonah have free will? Was some higher force capable of making decisions that controlled Jonah's destiny?

Jonah decided to test this hypothesis. He would repeat his experiment on observing the racquet balls, but this time he would alter the rules. He would kill himself unless *all* the hits fell on the left wall over a ten-second period of time. There was only a minimal possibility within the realm of quantum mechanics that this event would occur. But if this highly unlikely event occurred at this particularly meaningful time, he would reconsider the idea that there was a higher level ENTITY that had some idea of saving him. Let that ENTITY arrange *all* the hits this time to fall on the left side. Then he would be more convinced that he ought to stay put and not commit suicide. He would even begin to think that there was something about this Entity that he would even bring himself to call—GOD. Jonah began to observe the racquet balls. After ten seconds it was apparent that each wall had absorbed about half the hits. The disappointment of the outcome overwhelmed Jonah, and he decided irrevocably that this was the end for him. There was no God. There was no meaning.

Jonah was about to submerge his head in the digestive acid when just then the whale surfaced. With a wrenching contraction of its digestive apparatus, it forcefully expelled Jonah into the ocean.

CHAPTER 13.

JONAH DREAMS OF CREATION AND THE EVOLUTION OF THE UNIVERSE AND MORALITY.

Is There Purpose in the World?

Jonah spun about, and in the moments of his panic he saw flash before him a picture of the evolution of the universe. Conscious quarks arose from nothing and by their interactions formed space, time, matter, all in conscious form. Unique atmospheric conditions, in at least one planet within trillions of galaxies, allowed complex molecules to develop, some with the ability to reproduce. The most adaptive molecules survived and through further adaptation formed ever more complex organisms. Motivated by self-survival instincts, organisms focused on activities that promoted their own survival, without regard to the interests of other organisms of the species. It proved of greater survival value to the species, however, if each organism acted for the good of the species rather than directing its behavior solely toward its own survival.

In some species, this group concern developed rather early. Certain ant colonies had many members that were willing to fight for the group rather than run away for self-protection and let the others fight. In the human and many other species, this group instinct became manifest in at least one highly noticeable way — maternal instinct. A mother would be highly protective of its young despite great danger to herself. People eventually realized that for their own individual welfare it was best for them to form common laws to live by. People gave up their right to kill and steal in exchange for laws of society that protected everyone. By conceding to such societal laws, the individual, while giving up something, gained even more in the way of protection. Survival of the species worked best when individuals cooperated for the good of the group. Still, the motivation to act for the group's benefit was to a large degree motivated by self-interest. I.e., one acted for the group's benefit because he felt that in the end it would benefit him. This situation was not ideal, however, for there were many instances where one could deduce that acting for one's own immediate benefit might have greater benefit to one's self than acting toward the group's benefit. Sacrificing one's self in battle was one example. Evolution proceeded, however, to produce, on a genetic basis, certain individuals who had genuine concern for the group. There concern was as genuine as the maternal instinct. Just as certain animal species were intrinsically docile and others aggressive, some people had genuine intrinsic concern for others. Still others acquired such concern, not genetically, but through education. They were imprinted very early in their education with the idea that there was "good" and "evil." "Good" involved acting out of concern for others, and "evil" involved acting solely out of self-interest.

The world then broke up into two camps. In one camp, people were group-oriented, interested in the *group*. Decisions by the ruling body were made according to how they affected the group as a whole. This led to problems. Individuals could be killed for the sake of the group. The mentally retarded, the old, and eventually all sorts of people who in one way or another were considered a hindrance to society were disposed of. This did not sit well with the population. No one knew whether he or she would be next on the disposal list. If everyone were group-oriented, the plan might have worked, but most people retained vestiges of self-interest.

The other camp also was ruled by people who had the interest of the group in mind. But there was a variation to this theme. A person's concern was not for the group as a *whole*, but for other *individuals* in the group. Each person was respected as an individual and was special. Laws were made with the interest of the individual in mind rather than the nondescript group. This camp did much better. It was also composed of individuals who engaged in concern for others out of self-interest, and others who acted this way out of genuine concern for others, and still others who acquired the trait through education.

An inner voice then arose within Jonah in the form of a forceful idea. "Go and spread this message: Engage in activities for the good of others. In doing so, you will achieve benefits for yourself beyond those that you might at first suppose. Of course, there is the immediate benefit of increasing the probability that other people will react favorably toward you in return. But there is more. Every person eventually dies. What the person leaves behind are the innumerable effects of that person's influences in the world during his or her lifetime. That influence may be diffusely spread, but it is a form of information and a consciousness in itself, and it reflects the essence of that individual's actions. The individual will persist in this world even after his death by virtue of this conscious remnant. Separation in space and time of this influence on others does not affect the unified aspect of this consciousness. A brain that was theoretically divided into individual components that communicated over far distances would still retain its conscious unity. So does the information, and hence consciousness, that is associated with the result of that individual's lifetime of actions, persist as a conscious reflection of the self. Act for the benefit of others, and you will not only increase the likelihood of a reward to yourself in many cases while you are alive, but the positive effects of those actions will persist as part of your consciousness even after you die. Moreover, as one's consciousness exists everywhere at all times, there are innumerable other existences as well. In these existences, repeated emphasis on the welfare of others will, as a net result, assure, rather than just increase, the likelihood of your happiness."

As Jonah struggled with the waves, a series of disconnected and nonsensical images flashed through his mind. He saw himself in a large gambling hall, seated next to a blackjack player. The player was winning. Jonah asked him the secret of his success. After all, wasn't blackjack just gambling, in which the odds were stacked against him? Even a good blackjack player could not expect to win even half of the hands.

"Yes, replied the blackjack player. I do win a little less than half the hands, but I still come out ahead, because I know which hands I am likely to win, and I bet more at those times. You see, every time the dealer deals, I remember the cards, keeping track of those cards remaining in the deck. As the dealer continues to deal, I know what remains in the deck. Knowing the remaining cards gives me an edge; I know if the remainder of deals are more likely or less likely to be in my favor. If they are not in my favor, I bet less. If they are in my favor I bet more. I still come out ahead, even though I win fewer than half of the hands. This is called 'card-counting.' It is not looked upon with favor with the administrators of this establishment." That this was true became apparent when, following several nods among several key bouncers, Jonah and the blackjack player were promptly thrown from the building.

In the confusion, a giant series of random numbers paraded before Jonah: 3141592653589793238462643383279502884. . . . ., and then another number, 6920443710819621278638824. . . . . ., and then a third set of numbers, 8031554821930732389749935. . . . . ., For a brief moment Jonah was given the opportunity to experience all the consciousness in the universe at once. He was nearly deafened by the silence. Then he lost consciousness.

CHAPTER 14.

JONAH CONVERSES WITH AN INNER VOICE.

Why Do Bad Things Happen To Good People? What is the Purpose of Jonah? What is the End of Evolution?

Jonah found himself on the shore. Playful little waves stimulated and refreshed his body. In his immediate euphoria at being saved, he set out to spread his message of peace at a nearby village that was not especially known for peacefulness. Seeing the utilitarian aspect of the argument, the city occupants actually listened. Each person within the city began to act with respect for each other person in the city. Admittedly, though, the people were easier to convince than one might have first imagined because the sailors on Jonah's ship had already reached the city and told the occupants about the strange events that befell Jonah. Thus, the occupants already held Jonah in some sort of mystical regard.

Jonah then left the city. It was unbearably hot and Jonah sat down, greatly oppressed by the heat.

A giant gourd grew up around Jonah, providing him with a soothing shade. Exhausted, Jonah slept. In this dream, Jonah dreamed of God. What was God, and if God existed, what relationship did He have to Jonah?

Jonah came to believe in some kind of a unity, some primary equation, perhaps, for the formation of the universe, from which everything arose. The unity was not just the mathematical equation, but the significance of the equation, the consciousness that sprang from the information within that equation, everything in the universe that that equation symbolized. This not only included the things that the human mind is capable of experiencing, but also conscious experiences that lie beyond the capacity of the human mind.

The Unity of the universe was impossible for anyone to grasp, as there was too much knowledge for any one person to absorb. And even if that knowledge could be obtained, one could not be conscious of the whole even in a lifetime of thought, as our true consciousness is defined in terms of our ability to convey that information to others. One could never have a state of the brain that was capable of transmitting all that information, even in a lifespan. Moreover, our brains could not focus on all elements of that information, to narrow down and contemplate what a subdivision of "green" might be, all the way down to a conscious quark.

It was conceivable, though, that one could *feel* the presence of such a Unity. One can contemplate a house without seeing the bricks. One can contemplate "red" without seeing its postulated quark-like roots. One could contemplate, experience, feel the Unity without understanding the underlying structural elements that led to such a higher hierarchical experience, just as an idiot savant may successfully multiply large numbers mentally, without being able to tell us how he did it.

Jonah defined in his own mind that Unity of the universe as being God. He looked upon a universe that was created out of zero. Was his view so heretical? Did this view deny the existence of an everexisting God? If by zero, one meant the absence not only of matter but also of space and time, then God, while being created out of nothing, had been here since the beginning of time.

Was Jonah's vision of evolution of human society at odds with the point of view that had God, rather than natural evolution, being the force for morality in the world? Good will toward one's fellow person was the final goal in Jonah's scheme of evolution. Was this not the same goal desired by God? Could Jonah have been thinking about God all along, but in different terms—a Unity that was infinite, that existed since the beginning of time, yet was consistent with the laws of physics. There was even room in Jonah's scheme of things for the presence of morality, free will and the intervention of a higher order in the affairs of the universe. If people had free will (the belief in the latter being a leap of faith), should not God's mind, which is made of the same stuff as human consciousness but at a higher hierarchical level, also exhibit free will? God to Jonah was synonymous with the implications of a Grand Unified probablistic equation for the universe.

At daybreak Jonah received some bad news. The occupants of the city, while caring for one another within their own group, had banded together into a strongly unified group that had little regard for other groups. They were planning to attack Jonah's own city. This discouraged Jonah greatly. He had meant well but only brought on troubles for his own group. How he hated that other city, now.

Moreover, a worm began eating its way through the gourd and destroyed it, leaving Jonah exposed once again to the harsh rays of the sun. Whereas one can at times in life bear up to the frustration of a single disappointment, there are times when the simultaneous occurrence of more than one misfortune can be overbearing.

Jonah was greatly distraught. His efforts had been in vain. While well-intentioned, he had done more harm than good in regard to his own city. Moreover, he had lost the gourd. Why had all these misfortunes occurred to him? Was he any worse than anyone else? If there were a "God" in this world why did he let bad things happen to good people? Innocent children born with deformities and fatal illnesses; victims of concentration camps. Could one really believe that God allows suffering because the people who suffer are bad? Jonah considered that those who made that claim surely presented an unjustified affront to those victims and to the survivors who mourned their loss. Was one to assume that there is a "God" who is bad, who doesn't care? Or that there is a "God" that is powerless to control events in the world? Perhaps there is no such "God" and Jonah's evolutionary, scientific world is not synonymous with God, for one would not *expect* Jonah's scientific world view to necessarily be endowed with any special qualities such as fairness and justice. There might be a certain *utility* in believing in God in that it gave people the idea that certain "good" behavior was mandatory and thereby force them into that mold, but having utility did not necessarily imply the *truth* of God's existence.

An inner voice then spoke to Jonah. This inner voice, or strong idea, arose partly from information acquired during Jonah's life experiences, and partly from information within his genome, acquired through heredity, its roots originating many years in the past. It was the voice of God.

INNER VOICE: Jonah. When people act out of respect and concern for others, they increase the probability that other people will be good to them and they thus increase the probability of being rewarded in this world.

JONAH: Yes, how simple and nice a view, but "probability" does not mean a certainty. Certainly the world is full of examples of people who tried their best to accomplish fine goals but experienced horrible suffering in response. Is that fair, to offer someone just a "probability" of reward?

INNER VOICE: Yes, it is, because one must take into account not only one's consciousness in this world, but the consciousness that persists after death. Information, and hence consciousness (your consciousness included) is spread throughout the universe and exists regardless of the presence of your body. There are many conscious existences. What is only a probability of reward in this existence becomes a certainty when considered in the overall context of an infinite number of opportunities for actions, not only within one existence, but in multiple existences. Fairness will be meted out in the long run in the presence of multiple existences. Moreover, even in this existence, consciousness persists after death in the form of the results of one's actions that diffuse out in innumerable ways within the world itself. What diffuses out is a form of information in itself and a form of active consciousness that persists. Do not despair over the present unhappy outcome of well-directed efforts. Keep to the task, and you will continue to increase the likelihood of success, if not within this existence, then within some other.

I am not powerless to act. In quantum mechanics, there is a small possibility that anything can happen, even things that one might call miracles, which are only natural events that occur within the outer fringes of probability. If there is free will, then there is also MY will at a higher level of hierarchical organization, at a higher level of consciousness. I can work miracles, but do not expect them to happen frequently. I can make someone better through prayer, but do not expect that prayer to be answered with any greater degree of frequency than quantum probabilities will allow. Do not expect all the hits of the racquet balls to occur only on the left side of the court. If prevention of a holocaust depends on a sequence of events to occur that are as improbable as all the hits of those racquet balls being made on only the left side, I can do that, I am omnipotent. I am a racquetball court and you are a racquetball court. Within our own respective realms, we can determine that the net number of strikes will be greater on one side of the court than on the other side within a given trial. But do not expect that result too often. Otherwise, the laws of probability will not be followed. Moreover, regarding your raquetball experiment, I do not always choose to jump in and rescue people who have acted foolishly. Then they will never learn not to act foolishly.

JONAH: But is that fair, sometimes balancing the quantum decision in one person's favor and other times balancing it in another's favor, creating a miracle for one person but not for another who is equally as worthy? Surely, for quantum equations to be truly random, there should be an equal number of occasions when the quantum decision-making results in a favorable (fair) outcome as well as an unfavorable (unfair) outcome?

INNER VOICE: Do not think that it is unfair that sometimes the quantum decision falls out unfavorably for some and unfavorably for others. In the long run things will balance out, if not in this existence, then in other existences. Moreover, the balance of outcomes in 50-50 decisions is not necessarily precisely equal in the long run, but only approximately equal. The balance of good and evil in the world is a delicate one and can be tipped slightly to one side within this world at any given moment and still remain within the domains of the quantum equation. That slight edge can be quite significant, however, if the outcome of that decision is great. The blackjack player, despite his playing with a 50-50 chance of winning a series of hands, still came out ahead, because he knew those times when he was more likely to win and thereby bet more when his chances were greatest. Although a set of quantum decision may have a 50-50 outcome, a single one of the decisions, made in the right context, can have a profound outcome on the world.

JONAH: You speak of free will and God's will as occurring within the framework of quantum decisions. How do I know that these quantum decisions, like the balls striking one wall or the other, reflect free will rather than randomness? If you examine the patterns of all quantum decisions, you will only find randomness as the basis for the result in any given trial.

INNER VOICE: Jonah, you should reconsider what is really meant by true "randomness." You cannot determine that something is random. What may appear to be random may have more significance than is apparent. The number 314159265358979. . . . . , which you envisioned on the way to shore and which seemed to be a random sequence, is actually the decimal calculation for pi (3.14. . . . . etc.), and pi is hardly a random entity. Hidden within things that appear to be random may be things that are not random at all. As for the numbers 692044371081962127863882 4. . . . . . . and 80315548219307323897499 35. . . . . . which on the surface appeared to be truly random, these will give the result 1111111111111111111. . . . . . when subtracted from one another. Any random event may not be random at all when compared with some second event that is outside the first event. And who can know all the events in the world so as to say that a particular event is truly random? The information associated with the Unity in the universe can influence individual events. But perhaps more important than any subtle interactions by Me at the quantum level, are the decisions that individuals make. Even without the quantum effect being influenced by My consciousness, it is a natural consequence of one's good actions over a long period of time that one will increase the likelihood of a favorable outcome.

JONAH: But why should you have to follow a probablistic equation? Why not override that equation and always mete out justice on the spot when it is indicated?

INNER VOICE: Because, Jonah, I *am* that probablistic Grand Equation and that is the way the equation operates. Do not think that minimizes the image of God by defining Him in terms of that equation. That equation has enormous ramifications, far more than the human mind could ever visualize. There *are* certain things that I cannot do. I cannot destroy Myself. I cannot destroy that equation.

Once again, Jonah drifted out of consciousness and into sleep. He dreamed of a future world in which teleportation was common. In the early days of the technique, one could instantly be teleported from, say, New York to San Francisco by a process that first involved the dissembly of one's body into component atoms. The numbers and patterns of those atoms were recorded and sent telegraphically over long distances where other atoms were reassembled to duplicate the same person's structure. The technique was highly accurate. At first, though, many people were reluctant to submit to this process, for the question arose as to whether or not the first stage of dissembly of the body constituted murder. After all, the original body (in New York) had to first disintegrate; then the new body (in San Francisco) was constructed of other atoms. Soon, however, people got over these fears and came to feel that there was no murder, for the original person, at least so far as his mind was concerned, did reappear in San Francisco. Thus, "murder" was O.K. if it were painless and the individual resurfaced.

Problems arose, however. A few cases occurred in which the teleportation process was unsuccessful, resulting in a dead person at one end and no resurfacing clone at the other end. This led scientists to modify the technique, as follows: The individual would not be dissembled. Rather, an instrument was constructed that took an elaborate map reading of the living individual and transported this information long distances, whereupon a twin was reconstructed. The original twin was then killed (painlessly). This at first produced far greater controversy than was the case for the original teleportation method. It seemed to many people that this method, which involved permanently killing a twin, was much closer to murder, and people at first were quite reluctant to submit to the technique. However, a certain other logic prevailed. After all, the technique was safer than the original method, for if the teleportation failed, one would not proceed to kill the original twin. And one simply could not allow the confusion that would certainly arise with the allowance of both twins to survive. The technique in time became accepted, although there were some difficulties that arose when the original twin was not killed immediately, but stayed around for several minutes after the transfer. In those instances, even though only several minutes had elapsed, this was sufficient time for each of the twins to develop into persons slightly different from one another. The original twin then had the uncomfortable notion that he would not be replaced exactly, but that someone slightly different from himself, i.e., someone that was not he, would take his place. Such fears eventually died out, too, for it was pointed out that we are always changing anyway, never the same from one moment to the next. Moreover, while not exactly the same, the second twin was close enough. In fact, many people actually wished for far greater differences between themselves and the newly formed twin; when their original selves had been unhappy, had undergone great personal-social, physical, or mental losses, they would be relieved to have a twin that experienced fewer of these misfortunes.

Jonah realized that the persistence of his mind, his soul, after death related to his vision of the twins. There would be many somewhat different Jonahs in existences that were similar. And there would be many somewhat different existences with Jonahs that were similar. These variations, when not extreme, did not destroy the entity that was and always would be "Jonah." In each existence, though, Jonah had the opportunity to improve his lot by proper actions, thereby increasing the chances of happiness for that diffuse composite Jonah-Being that resided in all the existences together. By striving toward good actions in each existence, Jonah would achieve reward in the totality of existences as a whole, even though he might not meet with success in any individual existence.

JONAH: I have failed in what I thought was my goal. If I continue to spread the same message to other cities, what guarantee will I have that I will not continue to spread more harm than good? What now shall I do with my life?

INNER VOICE: You must pursue your goal of contributing to civilization in the best way that you know. There is no guarantee of success in any particular existence, but there is something that needs to be added to your message in this world that will increase the chances of your own and everyone else's happiness. Review once again the aims of evolution.

You have correctly concluded that it is more adaptive to the world for individuals to act out of respect and concern for one another. But there is still something missing —a further stage in evolution that must occur. Many people have made great strides toward achieving part of the objective. There are communities with ministers who have achieved great closeness and cooperation and love within the family of their own community. When people within the community are in need, there are always others within the community who are there to help them. But many of those same ministers show only contempt for other communities. They protect their own but create great strife and unhappiness by despising others who are not within their own group. Evolution has a further goal that has not as yet been accomplished. *For the sake of survival of the species, evolution must advance to the point which encompasses not just concern and respect for individuals WITHIN one's own group, but concern and respect for those OUTSIDE the group as well.* This is the logical end result of evolution. If you wish to state this in others words, it is God's will, or whatever. It should be your will to adopt this goal and to try to carry it out within the range of your abilities, to carry the message and show it by your example.

Whether you call Me "God" or an evolutionary sequence operating within the framework of physical law, this makes no difference. You may feel that there is a difference, that belief in God *mandates* certain moral behavior, whereas the scientific view does not mandate that behavior. However, a belief in God does not mandate that anyone act in a certain way. Everyone under "God" has a choice as to whether or not to behave in a "good" manner. If they do, they increase their probability of reward. If they don't, they decrease this probability. The same is true of the scientific explanation of the universe in terms of the Grand Unified equation. By acting in certain ways that are adaptive to society, one increases one's chances of reward and decreases it by maladaptive behavior. These views of God and the universe are one and the same.

It was evening. Jonah looked at the stars that filled the clear sky. Ancients had pondered the stars, seeking in them patterns that would give some indication of purpose in the universe. Some envisaged mythological figures in the patterns of stars. Others placed great significance in the motions of planets. Jonah had always seen only randomness in the pattern, but now this randomness had special significance to him.

If this were a deterministic universe, he thought, and it arose from a single event of creation, why was not the pattern of stars in the heavens a highly symmetrical one? A big bang from a single unity in a deterministic universe should result in a symmetrical pattern. The randomness of the pattern was more consistent with a probablistic equation operating within the universe. Perhaps there was indeterminacy and free will, after all. Perhaps there was a God. Perhaps God did play dice and intervene in the world through probability. And if there were no God, or if there were a God who did not intercede, there was still the potential of a human free will that could make significant changes in this world and in other existences.

Jonah really did not know. He kept these options open. The presence of the options was more satisfying to him than the thought of a coldly deterministic world.

Jonah slept again and dreamed that he was given the opportunity to visit both heaven and hell. In hell he entered a large room in which people were sitting around a huge table on which there was a delicious banquet. The people's hands were chained to the table and the people could not partake in the banquet, because the forks were several feet long. Try as they may, they could not feed themselves; the forks were far too long to place the food in their mouths. People were miserable.

Jonah then visited heaven, and again entered a large banquet hall. There was the same arrangement - delicious food, people with their hands bound to the table, and very long forks. In this room, however, the people were very happy. Each person was easily feeding his neighbor across the table.

Jonah found a purpose in life. With free will, and perhaps a little bit of guidance from above, or perhaps a little bit of luck, he might accomplish something useful in his lifetime.

Jonah awoke and walked along the shore and thought. All these dreams. What was real? Presumably reality was the original world from which originated all his succession of dreams. But could the original world be a dream as well, a dream that was made from zero at the time of creation? Was his life just an imaginary story in someone's book? Has the present always been around?

Jonah lay down to rest. The roll and roar and rhythm of the waves echoed something from the far, far past, something powerful, something soothing, something cyclic, something secret. And Jonah slept.

CHAPTER 15.

SUMMARY

This book is an exploration of the definition, origins, and significance of consciousness.

1. What is consciousness? Consciousness, within the context of this book is defined as simple awareness, i.e. the color "red," the smell of "rose," the taste of "coffee," etc.

2. Why are certain areas of the brain called "conscious" and others not? Actually, all areas are conscious. The difference between the areas lies in their ability to let the outside world know about this consciousness. The whale was unaware of Jonah's thoughts, even though Jonah was within the whale and quite conscious. The seeming all-or-none quality of consciousness does not depend on reaching a threshold degree of complexity. Simple things are conscious, too, but to a lesser degree. Non-neuronal tissues are conscious; non-human tissues are conscious; for it is the *information* content, not the materials that carry that information that is responsible for consciousness. Thus, a computer can be conscious as well. What we have been used to calling "consciousness" is just that portion of consciousness that the person can relate to others. The "unconscious" is that portion of consciousness that the person cannot relate to others. Thus, all parts of the brain are really conscious but many are just incapable of communicating this to the outside. The cerebellum (considered an "unconscious" organ) is actually conscious, like Jonah in the whale; and just as the whale is unaware of Jonah's thoughts, the person is unaware of the cerebellum's consciousness. We are full of conscious Jonahs.

3. What happens to consciousness when one dies? It is information that determines consciousness, and there is infinite information everywhere, just as a solid block of wood contains the information for an infinite number of kinds of sculptures. That infinite information, and hence, infinite consciousness, includes one's own consciousness and is there both before, during, and after one's lifetime. A person's actions during his lifetime changes the world in many different ways that remain after the person's death as a sort of information, and hence, consciousness, that is reflective of the individual. That remnant of scatted information persists in a form that can still interact with the world.

4. What is it about *information* that is responsible for particular conscious experiences, such as the "color red" or the "taste of coffee"? An answer arises in considering the problem of the creation of the universe, which must include the creation of consciousness as well.

Physicists talk about the creation of space, time and matter and talk of elementary bodies ("quarks") that are primary and form the basic building blocks for matter. Scientists, however, seldom talk about how *consciousness* was created, how "red," "coffee taste," "smell of rose," etc., originated. These questions are simplified if the original creation was that of consciousness, which includes not only the basic sense perceptions, but also space, time, and matter, as conscious experiences. The outside world is consciousness and made of the same material as a dream or thought. I speculate here, as do physicists (who propose the existence of primary "quarks" during creation), that there is a primary "quark-like" unit of consciousness, rather than numerous primary roots of consciousness (such as taste, smell, vision, hearing, and touch). From this conscious quark there arises, by virtue of combinations of associations with itself, all the other entities of consciousness of a higher hierarchical level. The brain in its firing patterns, reproduces

much of this associational information, hence duplicating consciousness, as the associational relationships are what is critical
to consciousness.

5. Does free will exist? That is a leap of faith. The emergence of
the uncertainty principle in quantum theory suggests a nondeterministic universe. This allows for the *possibility* of free will
while not proving it.

6. Is there a God? The answer depends on one's definition of
God. In the context of this book, God is defined in terms of a
unified probablistic equation for the universe and its conse-
quences. This does not trivialize God; the ramifications of such
an equation, in the levels and complexities of information and
consciousness that it implies, is far more than the human mind
can comprehend. If quantum phenomena allow for the possibility of human free will, then quantum phenomena also allow for
the possibility of God's will operating at a higher hierarchical
level under similar principles.

7. Does the latter definition of God allow for the concepts of
good and evil, and reward and punishment in the world? It
does: On an evolutionary scheme, society tends to develop on
an adaptive basis toward a situation where survival is better in-
sured through the cooperation of individuals, and the concern
and respect of one individual for another. Acting in this manner
increases the *probability* of reward for those actions in this world,
but *insures* reward if one considers the presence of multiple existences, wherein what is just a *probability* in this existence becomes a *certainty* by virtue of the large sampling of trials in
different settings.

8. Is there purpose in this world? On an evolutionary basis,
there is purpose in the sense that things evolve toward a state
wherein there is greater chance of survival if people care about

one another, not just about other members in their own group, but about individuals in other groups as well. Behavior along this direction is the goal of evolution. Using others words, but meaning the same thing, this is God's will, and one's purpose.

APPENDIX I.

The Meaning of "I"

As sensory input reaches the brain and is stored, there are many associations that link the data in many ways. "Grass" becomes associated with "green," with "the ground," with the eyes that saw the grass. "The ground" becomes associated with "earth," with the hands that felt the earth, etc. *All* information becomes associated with the idea of the person's body, whether it is the nose that smelled the coffee, the eyes that saw the grass, the ears that heard the sound, the tongue that tasted the sugar, the finger that felt the pinprick, and most universally, with the person as a whole, who contains the nose, eyes, ears, tongue, and fingers. Thus, all information is associated in some way with information that relates to the person. That is the "I," the association with the person, which accompanies all conscious thoughts and which gives the person the feeling that his thoughts are uniquely his own.

APPENDIX II.

The Computer That Opted For Dualism

Once there was a computer with a simple mechanism for comparing the differences between different inputs. If a sound was presented to the computer, special sound sensors responded by activating pathways that led to gait A. Gait A then recorded the letter "S" (for "Sound") in its memory. If a light image was presented to the computer, this activated a light sensor that activated pathways that led to gait B. Gait B then put the letter "L" (for "Light") in its memory. The computer had a mechanism for comparing two inputs. If both inputs were "S" or both inputs were "L" then it responded by flashing on its screen "Inputs 1 and 2 are *the same.*" If one input was "S" and the other input was "L" it responded by flashing on its screen "Inputs 1 and 2 are *different.*"

On one occasion an observer presented the computer with the sound of a car honking. The computer registered "S" in its memory bank for this first input. All that the observer noted in this series of events was the fact that impulses raced down the computer circuit pathways to gait A, and from there went to the memory bank to register the letter "S." The observer then decided to present the computer with exactly this picture—an actual movie sequence of the impulses racing down the computer circuit pathways to gait A, and from there going to the memory bank to register the letter "S." Since this latter information was presented to the computer in the form of a picture, it activated the light sensor that activated pathways that led to gait B. Gait B then put the letter "L" in its memory and flashed on the screen "Inputs 1 and 2 are different." In other words, the computer appeared to indicate that the input of sound that it received was not the same as the events that occurred in its circuitry at the time. I.e., the totality of events that occurred in its circuitry at the time that the sound was presented was not equivalent to its experience of the sound itself. The computer opted for a dualistic point of view.

This is not to say that the computer was actually conscious of sound. It merely shows how some sort of dualism can be arrived at, even by a computer, as it tries to analyze whether the information that its circuitry processes is identical to the events that are going on in its circuitry. It would appear that these things should be one and the same, but the computer concludes otherwise.

Does not a similar phenomenon occur in humans, when trying to contemplate how a particular conscious feeling can be equivalent to the events going on in the person's circuitry? We inevitably must conclude that there are a mind and a body, even though all that is occurring is firing of circuitries. We come to this false conclusion, partly, because, in trying to analyze the "information" in the circuitries, we inevitably throw into the analysis the vehicles that carry that information, namely the protoplasm and the mathematical symbols that carry the information. These are different from the information itself.

Moreover, even if we could somehow succeed in separating the actual information from the vehicles that carry the information, there are other reasons why we conclude that there is a dualism. Any input that enters the information processing mechanisms in our brains inevitably is distorted in some way (e.g., in tacking on the conscious idea of "visible, the eyes" on viewing something). If we try to analyze the final product (that is, the information from the viewed object plus the added information of "visible, the eyes") then the very act of trying to picture the information changes that information again, leading to something different from the original information that was processed. Moreover, if code X is presented to the brain and the brain acts to transcribe it into code Y, then presenting the brain with code Y will cause the brain to convert that code Y to some other form of code Y (Y′) which is not the same as Y.

Try as we may, even if we were capable of separating the pure information in our brains from the vehicles that carry that information, the very process of analyzing that information distorts it so as to force us to conclude that there is a dualism. Even a computer would do that.

APPENDIX III.

Quantum Phenomena and Consciousness

The question of the nature of human consciousness arises frequently in the interpretation of quantum phenomena, as in the wave-particle controversy. The following is a brief summary of this controversy.

In the classic double slit experiment (fig. 2), light (or in fact any small particles, such as electrons) is aimed at a double slit. The resulting pattern on the screen that lies beyond is an interference pattern of the kind indicating some sort of wave inter-

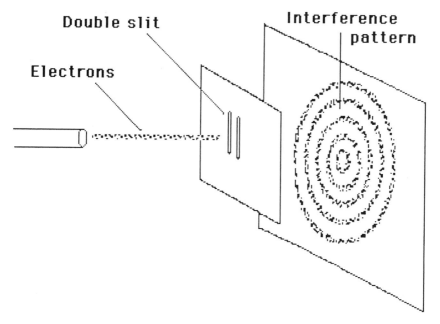

Fig. 2 The wave-particle phenomenon. Electrons, or other particles, when shot individually through a double slit, result in a screen pattern suggestive of wave interference.

ference. The interference pattern would lead one to suppose that such small particles are actually waves, as the interference pattern is best explained by a wave hitting the two slits at once, and then breaking up into two waves which would then interfere with one another beyond the slits. Even if electrons are aimed one at a time at the double slit, the resulting pattern is an interference pattern. If light or electrons were just particles, then each particle would pass through either of the two slits and give rise to a pattern on the screen that would not have alternating lines as would be the case for an interference pattern.

The problem that arises is that in some aspects, light and electrons do appear to act as discreet particles. One dramatic way that this can be seen is in the straight line track of an electron that travels through an experimental cloud chamber. The particulate nature is in fact also seen even in the double slit experiment if one uses a screen in which single grains of photographic emulsion deposit with each electron that strikes the screen. For instance, if a single electron is allowed to pass through the slit apparatus and strikes the screen, what will appear is a solitary dot of developed emulsion on the screen, rather than a diffuse pattern of developed silver grains. As each successive electron reaches the screen, more and more dots form on the screen, until a final pattern is arrived at. That final pattern is one of rings, the same pattern that would occur on aiming many electrons at once at the slits.

The paradox in the wave-particle controversy, then, is that on the one hand the electron appears to be a particle (individual dots on the screen). On the other hand the electron appears to be a wave (the interference pattern).

In the situation in which one electron at a time is aimed at the slits, the net result of each trial is a single grain of silver depositing on the screen. Where exactly it hits (e.g., to the right or the left side of the screen) is believed to be a random process. Most physicists today believe that the random nature of the strikes is truly random and not due to hidden variables among the particles that cause one particle to behave differently from another.

Many other kinds of quantum events are also believed to be "random." In the phenomenon of radioactive decay, for instance, each radioactive substance has its own peculiar half life, the time which it takes for half of its decay. Why half of the particles should decay by that half time and the other half should not is believed to be due to a true randomness at the quantum level rather than to hidden variables among the particles. However, there are difficulties in pinpointing exactly what randomness is.

How can something be both a particle and a wave at the same time? One way is to consider that reality itself is determined by the means of observation. Prior to the time that the decision was made as to which measuring device to use, there is no reality of either a particle or a wave. The method of observation determines the reality of the event. We determine what reality is according to which method of observation that we use. If we choose to use a particle detector (e.g., a cloud chamber), then the reality is that of a particle. If we use an interference detector (e.g., a double slit setup), what exists is a wave. Until the time that the actual recording is made and the results of the experiment are finalized, the wave versus particle nature is indeterminate, both practically and theoretically. This interpretation has led some people to believe that there is something mystically strange about the phenomenon of human consciousness, that, somehow, reality is dependent on the fixation of an event in human consciousness, and that consciousness creates reality. This interpretation, however, inevitably leads to the paradox known as "Schroedinger's Cat."

Irwin Schroedinger, one of the founders of quantum mechanics, imagined a live cat inside a closed box. A quantum decision, namely, whether or not a particular quantum particle will undergo radioactive decay, is about to happen in the box. If the decay occurs, this will set into action a device that will kill the cat. If the decay does not occur, then the cat lives. Does the cat die or not? One does not know until one opens the box. If reality of the decay depends on the observation, then the reality of whether or not the cat is alive (which is a macroscopic, not just a quantum event) is not set until the box is opened. One could not say that some decision as to the cat's fate was already determined prior to opening the box. The indeterminacy of the cat's status was not just the practical one of not knowing. There actually would be no reality to either the cat being alive or dead until the box is opened, as there was no reality of the quantum event until the box was opened. Thus indeterminacy at the quantum level could be extended into the macroscopic realm, and reality would be *dependent on one's conscious observation.* However, the problem with this reasoning, insofar as consciousness is concerned, is that one can readily imagine a human observer actually opening the box and seeing what the cat's status was. One would presume that this brought the reality of the situation into existence. However, what if that observer were himself in a still larger box that encompassed everything, and a second observer had to open that larger box to find out what the first observer had experienced? Then, from the point of view of the second observer, the event would be indeterminate until he opened that larger box. Events would be indeterminate even though a human observer (the first observer) had already been consciously involved with the observation.

The hypothesis that requires human consciousness for reality to occur does not fit well with such a thought experiment. From the point of view of this book, that idea certainly does not gel, as consciousness is not considered to be strictly a human property, but is associated with everything. An advanced computer that observed that same event would have just as good a hold on reality as would a human.

An alternative explanation is that the observer does not determine reality. The observer *discovers* reality rather than *invent* it.

Fig. 3   The figure ground. Is it a vase or two facial profiles?

There is an independent reality to the wave-particle that makes sense mathematically but is just difficult to visualize, in the same way that one cannot picture a fourth dimension. It is like the blind men examining the elephant. The person examining the front end cannot explain how the person examining the rear end should come to such a radically different view about what an elephant is. In reality, the elephant consists of both a front and a rear, and more. Similarly the electron may be something more than a wave and/or a particle, something that we have difficulty in visualizing, except in mathematical terms.

Consider the observation of a figure-ground picture (fig. 3). Is it a vase or two facial profiles? Say that the picture were locked in a box and two robots were sent in to investigate what was inside. One robot reported "figure" and the other "ground." Without having seen the picture, a person would have great difficulty in understanding how such separate conclusions could be drawn. The wave-particle may be like the figure-ground picture. We have never seen the total picture, but wave and particle may exist as part of that picture. Our brains have just not acquired sufficient information as to be able to picture what a wave-particle might look like, in the same way that we have difficulty in picturing a fourth dimension.

APPENDIX IV.

The Turing Machine and Computer Consciousness

Could a computer exhibit conscious intelligence? Alan Turing, one of the pioneers in computer development proposed a test, subsequently referred to as the Turing test, for conscious intelligence in computers. The test consists of placing the computer in a separate room from the observer, so that the observer does not know whether he is communicating with a real person or with a computer. The observer would then pose to the computer any question he or she wished. The computer would respond. The point is whether the computer would be able to fool the person into thinking that it was a human being responding. If the observer, after extensive interrogation of the computer, could not distinguish the computer's response from that of a person, then the computer would be said to have the ability to think like a person.

Actually, there are two points in question here. One is whether that computer could exhibit the intellectual thought processes of a person. The other is whether those thought processes are conscious. It is possible to conceive of a computer that exhibited perfect human-type responses to all questions, yet is still not conscious. There really is no reason to believe that a computer, theoretically, given enough information, could not duplicate human responses to all manner of questions. We will be concerned with whether a computer could exhibit *conscious* thought processes.

The Turing test is an exercise in inductive reasoning. No one can ever say for sure that a particular computer is conscious. A person can not even prove that any other person is conscious! One induces the latter from the knowledge that one person resembles people in many respects—anatomically, behaviorally, etc. Presumably, if I am conscious, other people are, too. Similarly, it is a best guess only, that if a computer responds like a human being, and, for our psychological purposes, it also was made to look like a human being, that it also exhibits consciousness.

Everyone knows, however, that inductive reasoning can be wrong. The proverbial chicken that believes it will always be fed because it has been fed every day, is proven quite wrong when the farmer kills it. If one could stop the sun, then our inductive reasoning that states that the sun will always rise, because we have always observed that, would be wrong. Similarly, one can cleverly devise a situation in which a computer (or a person) will give answers identical to those of a normal human being, yet not be conscious of the significance what it (he) is saying. For example, if a person (or computer) who did not understand Chinese, memorized all the proper verbal responses, in Chinese, to any Chinese question posed to it, the answers would appear to an observer who understood Chinese to be reflective of an individual who knew full well what he was talking about, even though the speaker had no idea of the meaning of the words (*), and would even say so outright.

All this means is that the Turing test is not infallible. Any exercise in inductive reasoning may be fallible. The person who memorized the Chinese responses could not know that a particular word meant "house," because there are no associations in his brain circuitries that link the information of the Chinese word for "house" with the information of the visual experience of a house. When asked whether or not he understood what was being said, the person would say that he did not, that it was all just a jumble of meaningless words to him. If the person, or computer, did indeed have linkage of the word "house" with the information of a picture of a house, then both person and com-

---

*Searle, John R., Minds, Brains, and Programs, in *The Mind's I*, ed. by D. R. Hofstadter and D. C. Dennett, pp. 353–373, Bantam Books, 1981.

puter would be fully conscious of the picture of the house when contemplating the Chinese word for house. Simply presenting the Chinese word, i.e., symbol, for "house" is insufficient. That symbol needs further definition in terms of other symbols that are not simply words, but interrelationships of a coherent picture of house. With that further definition, the person, when presented with the Chinese word, will then draw the picture of the house, to illustrate his consciousness of house, and state that he is conscious of it. (This does not necessarily mean that the information for the picture of "house" has to include all the root information down to the elementary quark of consciousness. Just as one can conceive of a house without understanding the composition of the bricks, one might, without having to include the quark roots of consciousness, picture to some degree, the conscious image of a house, as long as there are at sufficient numbers of subdivided symbols to represent the actual house).

Showing fallibility in the Turing test does not show, as has been purported, that computers could not eventually be developed that think consciously like people. Such fallibility in the Turing test simply shows that the test is not necessarily a reliable indicator of consciousness. Based on the reasoning in this book, it is more rational to believe that today's computers are indeed conscious, but to such an *elementary* degree as to be incomprehensible to us, but that they could, in principle, advance to much higher states of consciousness, approaching that of humans or beyond, given sufficient sophistication in their information makeup and processing. It is not protoplasm, as opposed to wires, that makes consciousness. *It is the information content.* Numerous studies on the brain, to date, indicate that the key function of the brain's underlying biochemistry and anatomy is to make the brain an efficient information processor, which acts to receive information, integrate it, store it, and transfer it to other brain areas, or out of the brain to other areas. Consciousness occurs in the process. And so it should in a machine that duplicated the same information processing.

peor would in fully convinced of his picture of the house when demonstrating the Chinese word for house. Simply presenting the Chinese word, the symbol for "house," is insufficient; that symbol needs further definition to remove ambiguities that are not simply words, but intermediate, here more current phenomena in nouns. With further definition the person when presented with the Chinese word will then have the picture of the house, reflecting his consciousness of house." And such, then he is conscious of it. (But does not the mentalism from the intuition, the meaning of "house" has already, in the last thing into itself, some element as a speech of representationwise, as no one can imagine of a house when undertaking the examination that asks when such a kind of undertaking to develop the quiet mind's consciousness, picture to approaching the reaching stage of a further and so is then total sufficient processing that vividly evidence to represent the alternate of the same ultimately acute during the feature this far show, as has been pointed out that to equiment could not eventually be level that when consciously the principle to Philosophy in the living it so simply show that the field is not necessarily a reliable indication of consciousness, based on the reminding in this work it is more rational to believe that today's computers indeed can account to reach such consciousness as reached to be the computers can just tell that they could, imperceptible, assume to which a particular to consciousness, approaching that of human mentality, would prove sufficient subjectation in the conscious the mind and processes. It's no protoplasm, as opposed to which until certain consciousness; it's the mentation appear, but perhaps similar to the brain, to our brain, that the key function of the brain's underlying biochemistry, and analogous to make the brain, an effort, of more fully process, which acts to receive information and guide it through and brain in the other functions, output of the brain to phenomena. Consciousness' output and process. And such should up a machine that duplicated the same mentation processing.